Table of Contents

History from the Beginning

1.   What was the world's first nuclear powered submarine? USS *Nautilus*

2.   Counting Pope Francis, how many Popes have there been? 266

3.   Which World War II battle is officially called The Ardennes Offensive? Battle of the Bulge

4.   How many delegates signed the Declaration of Independence? 56

5.   Who was the first person to reach the North Pole? Robert Peary

6.   In what year was the Cuban Missile Crisis? 1962

7.   Ernesto 'Che' Guevara died in which country? Bolivia

8.   Who is the only person to have been the recipient of two unshared Nobel Prizes? Linus Pauling

9.   Who was the first woman to be awarded the Distinguished Flying Cross? Amelia Earhart

10. What Mexican leader was assassinated in 1923? Pancho Villa

11. What was the world's first electrically lighted city? Wabash, Indiana

12. What U.S. Navy destroyer was the victim of a terrorist attack on October 12, 2000? USS *Cole*

13. What political figure was born Vladimir Ilich Ulyanov? Lenin

14. How many Confederate states were there during the U.S. Civil War? 11

15. In 1813, Simon Bolivar became President of which country? Venezuela

16. Ishtar Gate served as one of the entrances to what ancient city? Babylon

17. Which World War II leader was born on July 29, 1883? Benito Mussolini

18. Which emperor of the Roman Empire's name meant, Little Soldier's Boot? Caligula

19. In 1517, who nailed *The 95 Theses* onto the door of the Palace Church of Wittenberg? Martin Luther

20. Who was the United States' first multi-millionaire? John Jacob Astor

21. Which former U.S. state governor was born James George Janos? Jesse Ventura

22. Who was the first woman in space? Valentina Tereshkova

23. Ferdinand Porsche designed which car that was launched in 1937? Volkswagen Beetle

24. Who killed Billy the Kid? Sheriff Pat Garrett

25. Who was the first female U.S. Secretary of State?
Madeleine Albright

26. In what year was the U.S. *Monroe Doctrine* introduced?
1823

27. Which U.S. state was first to elect a woman to
Congress? Montana

28. Which African leader is the only person in history to
have addressed both the League of Nations and the
United Nations? Haile Selassie I

29. Tenochtitlan was the capital of which empire? Aztec

30. Who shot and killed Jesse James? Robert Ford

31. Who was King Arthur's wife? Guinevere

32. Who attempted to assassinate Edwin (Ted) Walker on
April 10, 1963? Lee Harvey Oswald

33. What was the first state to ratify the U.S. Constitution?
Delaware

34. Who was the first U.S. Vice President to resign from
office? John C. Calhoun

35. Who did FBI agents shoot outside Chicago's Biograph
Theater on July 22, 1934? John Dillinger

36. Who was the mother of King James 1 of England?
Mary, Queen of Scots

37. Who was the first emperor of the Holy Roman Empire?
Otto I

38. In what year was the summit of Mount Everest first reached? 1953

39. Who was U.S. Vice President under Abraham Lincoln? Andrew Johnson

40. In what year did the Gunfight at the O.K. Corral take place? 1881

41. Harald Bluetooth was king of which country? Denmark

42. How many Dalai Lamas have there been? 14

43. In what country was Nostradamus born? France

44. The end of the Pony Express was in which California town? Sacramento

45. Which Carthaginian general led his army across the Alps with elephants? Hannibal

46. What was the first U.S. state with speed limit signs? Oregon

47. How many years did Nelson Mandela spend in prison before his release in 1990? 27

48. Which emperor's personal sword was named Joyeuse? Charlemagne

49. Who was Vice President of the Confederate States of America? Alexander H. Stephens

50. In what present day country was the Battle of Waterloo fought? Belgium

51. In what year was the Battle of Hastings? 1066

52. In what year did construction of the Berlin Wall begin? 1961

53. Charge of the Light Brigade occurred during which war? Crimean War

54. Who assassinated Robert Kennedy? Sirhan Sirhan

55. In 1980, which U.S. city presented Saddam Hussein with a key to the city? Detroit

56. Which British monarch was the last Emperor of India? George VI

57. In 1952 Albert Einstein was offered the presidency of which country? Israel

58. What is the first name of General Stonewall Jackson? Thomas

59. The Varangian Guard served and protected the rulers of what empire? Byzantine Empire

60. In 1986, the People Power Revolution took place in which country? Philippines

61. Which country has the oldest national flag? Denmark

62. Which plane was nicknamed the Flying Fortress in World War II? B-17

63. Who was the first person to receive Honorary U.S. Citizenship? Winston Churchill

64. In 1989, what trade union was legalized in Poland? Solidarity

65. What was J. Edgar Hoover's final year as Director of the FBI? 1972

66. Lebanon declared independence from which country in 1943? France

67. How many U.S. Presidents have been assassinated? 4

68. How many operational space shuttles were built by NASA? 5

69. Who was the first person to break the sound barrier? Chuck Yeager

70. Which empire lasted from 1324 to 1922? Ottoman Empire

71. Who was the last Tudor monarch? Queen Elizabeth I

72. What author recited his own poem "The Gift of Outright" at President John F. Kennedy's inauguration? Robert Frost

73. What was Operation Overlord? Invasion of Normandy

74. Which historical American was born Malcolm Little in 1925? Malcolm X

75. Who did Eva Braun marry in April of 1945? Adolf Hitler

76. Who was the first woman to swim the English Channel? Gertrude Ederle

77. In 1901, Albert Einstein became a citizen of which country? Switzerland

78. What is former U.S. Presidential candidate Mitt Romney's first name? Willard

79. What did archaeologist Hiram Bingham discover in 1911? Machu Picchu

80. What religion was founded by Prince Gautama Siddhartha? Buddhism

81. What university is home to the oldest medical school in the United States? University of Pennsylvania

82. What organization was founded in 1966 by Huey Newton and Bobby Seale? Black Panther Party

83. Who was the first American to orbit the Earth? John Glenn

84. What was the first U.S. military academy to admit women? U.S. Coast Guard Academy

85. How long did the Hundred Years' War last? 116 years

86. Who was the first woman to win a Nobel Prize? Marie Curie

87. Who was the only U.S. Congressman to vote against entering World War II? Jeanette Rankin

88. Marie Antoinette was married to which French King? Louis XVI

89. In what year did Mount St. Helens have its last major eruption? 1980

90. In which year was Alaska admitted as the 49th U.S. state? 1959

91. What was the original use of the Leaning Tower of Pisa? Bell tower

92. Who was Henry VIII's first wife? Catherine of Aragon

93. In 1988, which singer was elected Mayor of Palm Springs, California? Sonny Bono

94. How many people have walked on the moon? 12

95. Who was the last English king to die in battle? King Richard III

96. What was Socrates forced to drink to commit suicide? Hemlock

97. Who was known as the Maid of Orléans? Joan of Arc

98. In 1893, what country was the first to grant women the right to vote? New Zealand

99. General Franco was dictator of which country? Spain

100. What did all members of the Nazi SS have tattooed on their armpits? Their blood type

101. On what date did Neil Armstrong walk on the Moon? July 20, 1969

102. King Zog was the ruler of which country? Albania

103. What is the oldest Catholic university in the United States? Georgetown

104. Which U.S. Constitutional Amendment granted women the right to vote? 19th Amendment

105. In what year was the Selective Service Act enacted? 1917

106. Who was the first person in space? Yuri Gagarin

107. What kind of doctor was Doc Holliday? Dentist

108. In what year did World War I start? 1914

109. What is the name of the Russian mystic who was killed in December, 1916? Grigori Rasputin

110. What country landed on Juno Beach during D-Day? Canada

111. In what year was Amnesty International founded? 1961

112. What ship rescued the surviving passengers of RMS *Titanic*. RMS *Carpathia*

113. Who was the teacher who died when space shuttle *Challenger* exploded? Christa McAuliffe

114. Who was the father of Cleopatra's twins? Mark Antony

115. Who was the first to sail around the Cape of Good Hope? Vasco De Gamma

116. What was the first country to recognize the United States as a nation? Morocco

117. In what year was the Magna Carta created? 1215

118. In what year was the United States Secret Service founded? 1865

119. Aboard what ship did the Japan surrender to the U.S. and thus ending World War II? USS *Missouri*

120. Who was *Time* magazine's first Man of the Year in 1927? Charles Lindbergh

121. Who is the only person to have been executed by an Israeli civilian court? Adolf Eichmann

122. Which country is currently ruled by the Chakri Dynasty? Thailand

123. Who replaced Winston Churchill as Prime Minister of the United Kingdom in 1945? Clement Attlee

124. In what year did the first Gulf War take place? 1991

125. Who was the first African American featured on a U.S. postage stamp? Booker T. Washington

126. In what year did the Exxon Valdez cause a huge oil spill off the coast of Alaska? 1989

127. How old was Queen Elizabeth II at her coronation? 27

128. In what year was the storming of the Bastille in Paris? 1789

129. Who succeeded Nikita Khrushchev as Secretary of the Central Committee of the Communist Party of the Soviet Union? Leonid Brezhnev

130. In what year did the Battle of the Alamo take place? 1836

131. Where did General Robert E. Lee surrender to General Ulysses S. Grant to end the U.S. Civil War? Appomattox Court House, Virginia

132. Is what year did the United States celebrate its centennial? 1876

133. Who is the only U.S. Supreme Court Justice to be impeached? Samuel Chase

134. In what year did the *Mayflower's* pilgrims land at Plymouth Rock? 1620

135. David Ben-Gurion became prime minister of what country in 1948? Israel

136. Who became the leader of Kuomintang in 1926? Chiang Kai-shek

137. When did Margaret Thatcher become Prime Minister of the United Kingdom? 1979

138. In what year did the United States begin construction of the Panama Canal begin? 1904

139. What scandal was the Tower Commission set up to investigate in 1986? Iran-Contra Affair

140. What Pope had the shortest reign? Pope John Paul I

141. Who was vice president under President Dwight D Eisenhower? Richard Nixon

142. Who killed Alexander Hamilton in a duel? Aaron Burr

143. The Seven Weeks War was fought between Prussia and what other country? Austria

144. What U.S. military battle took place on June 25 & 26, 1876? Battle of the Little Bighorn

145. Who was Czar of Russia in 1917? Czar Nicholas II

146. What was the name of the first dog sent into space? Laika

147. Who became Prime Minister of the United Kingdom in 1937? Neville Chamberlain

148. In what year was the world's first nuclear bomb detonated? 1945

149. Who was the youngest signer of the Declaration of Independence? Edward Rutledge

150. What was the bloodiest single-day battle during the U.S. Civil War? Battle of Antietam

151. Who was the Democratic Party nominee for president in the 1860 election? Stephen Douglass

152. In what year was the Falklands War? 1982

153. What was the first permanent English settlement in the United States? Jamestown

154. In 1912, who became editor of the socialist newspaper *Avanti*? Benito Mussolini

155. In what year was the United States Marine Corp founded? 1775

156. What was the largest naval battle in world history? Battle of Leyte Gulf

157. During what war was the Battle of Heartbreak Ridge? Korean War

158. Who was the first African American U.S. Supreme Court Justice? Thurgood Marshall

159. In what year did the Manson Family kill actress Sharon Tate? 1969

160. In which U.S. state was the Klu Klux Klan founded? Tennessee

161. In what year did the Thirty Years' War end? 1648

162. Who did Rome fight against in the Punic Wars? Carthage

163. What is the name of battleship BB-39 that was sunk during the attack on Pearl Harbor? USS *Arizona*

164. Who piloted the *Spruce Goose* on its maiden flight? Howard Hughes

165. Who did then Prince Rainier of Monaco marry in 1956? Grace Kelly

166. Prathiba Patil was the first female President of which country? India

167. Who did Gavrilo Princip assassinate in 1914? Archduke Franz Ferdinand of Austria

168. Which Apollo 13 astronaut told Mission Control, "Houston, we've had a problem. We've had a Main B bus undervolt"? Jim Lovell

169. What holiday did Anna Jarvis start in 1907? Mother's Day

170. Atahualpa the last leader of which empire? Inca Empire

171. In what year did the Three Mile Island nuclear accident occur? 1979

172. Who was the last man to walk on the moon? Eugene Cernan

173. Who was the first African American U.S. Secretary of State? Colin Powell

174. Instead of the hand over heart, what was originally done during the Pledge of Allegiance? Bellamy Salute

175. Who was Ross Perot's running mate in the 1992 U.S. Presidential election? James Stockdale

176. During what war was the Battle of Bosworth Field fought? War of the Roses

177. In what year did the U.S. invade Grenada? 1983

178. Who was the first U.S. Attorney General? Edmund Randolph

179. What was the first U.S. college to admit females? Oberlin College

180. In what year did the Lockerbie bombing occur? 1988

181. During what war did the Gallipoli Campaign take place? World War I

182. Who was the only British Prime Minister to have been assassinated? Spencer Perceval

183. Who was the first U.S. Supreme Court Justice? John Jay

184. Who committed the world's first train robbery? Jesse James

185. Who was the first woman to appear on a U.S. postage stamp? Queen Isabella of Spain

186. What historical artifact did Pierre-François Bouchard find in 1799? Rosetta Stone

187. Which U.S. state had the first female governor? Wyoming

188. What was the first country to recognize same-sex marriages? The Netherlands

189. Who was the last emperor of Vietnam? Bao Dai

190. Who was Prime Minister of Great Britain during the French and Indian War? William Pitt

191. Which Pope had Napoleon Bonaparte excommunicated in 1809? Pope Pius VII

192. What was the first space shuttle launched in 1981? Columbia

193. Charles Curtis was the U.S. Vice President under which President? Herbert Hoover

194. Who was the first Emperor of the Roman Empire? Augustus

195. What was the first official legislative assembly in the Thirteen Original Colonies? House of Burgesses

196. Who was dictator of Cuba before being overthrown by Fidel Castro? Fulgencio Batista

197. Who was Amelia Earhart's in-flight navigator when her plane disappeared on July 2, 1937? Fred Noonan

198. Who created People's Temple? Jim Jones

199. Who was the last King of Rome? Lucius Tarquinius Superbus

200. In 1925, what teacher was put on trial for violating Tennessee's Butler Act? John Scopes

201. In what year was Charlemagne born? 742 A.D.

202. What empire was Mansa Musa ruler of from 1312-1337? Malian Empire

203. Who was King of England when William Wallace was captured in 1305? King Edward I

204. In which city did the 1999 WTO riots occur? Seattle, WA

205. What is the name of the airship that exploded over Lakehurst Naval Air Station on May 6, 1937? LZ 129 *Hindenburg*

206. During what war was the first Medal of Honor awarded? U.S. Civil War

207. Where did John Anglin, Frank Morris and Clarence Anglin escape from on June 11, 1962? Alcatraz Federal Penitentiary

208. What ruler had his son Alexei Petrovich sentenced to death? Peter the Great

209. What is the name of the plane Wilbur Wright flew on December 17, 1903? *Flyer*

210. What U.S. agency began operation on October 1, 1958? NASA

211. With the death of Duncan I, who became King of Scotland in 1040? Macbeth

212. Who was the last Roman Catholic King of England and Ireland? King James II

213. Who named his courtroom, The Jersey Lilly? Judge Roy Bean

214. In what year did the U.S. complete the Louisiana Purchase? 1803

215. In what year was gold discovered in California? 1848

216. Who was the first Czar of Russia? Ivan the Terrible

217. What Chinese leader was responsible for starting construction of the Great Wall of China? Qin Shi Huang

218. William Booth founded which organization in 1865? The Salvation Army

219. Who did Ramon Mercader assassinate? Leon Trotsky

220. What Pope was responsible for starting the First Crusade in 1095? Pope Urban II

221. On November 4, 1979, how many Americans were taken hostage in Iran? 52

222. In what year did the U.S. adopt "The Star Spangled Banner" as its official anthem? 1931

223. Who did the U.S. purchase the Virgin Islands from? Denmark

224. What was the 14th U.S. state to enter the union? Vermont

225. What nation gained its independence from Indonesia in 2002? East Timor

226. Who was King of Great Britain during the American Revolution? King George III

227. What U.S. submarine sank on April 10, 1963? USS *Thresher*

228. What couple was killed by law enforcement in Bienville Parish, Louisiana on May 23, 1934? Bonnie and Clyde

229. Which Apollo 11 astronaut did not walk on the moon? Michael Collins

230. Who was the longest-serving president in French history? Francois Mitterrand

231. Who was first female African American to go into outer space? Mae Jemison

232. Who did King Edward VIII marry after he abdicated in 1936? Wallis Simpson

233. Who was the first Chairman of the Joint Chiefs of Staff? General Omar Bradley

234. In what year did Prohibition end in the U.S.? 1933

235. Who was the first Prime Minister of India? Jawaharal Nehru

236. Who did Nelson Mandela share the 1993 Nobel Peace Prize with? F. W. de Klerk

237. Who was the last president of Czechoslovakia? Vaclav Havel

238. In what year was the United Nations founded? 1945

239. What U.S. Supreme Court decision set the principle of Judicial Review? *Marbury vs. Madison*

240. Members of what religious group were killed during the St. Bartholomew's Day Massacre in 1572? Huguenots

241. In what year was the dedication of the Statue of Liberty? 1886

242. Who was the first christian Emperor of Rome? Constantine the Great

243. What was the first submarine to sink an enemy warship? H.L. Hunley

244. In what year did the U.S. remove Manuel Noriega from power? 1989

245. Huey Long was governor of which U.S. state when he was assassinated in 1935? Louisiana

246. What was the first man-made structure to rise above 1,000 feet? Chrysler Building

247. What was the last name of the five brothers who all died during the sinking of *USS Juneau*? Sullivan

248. What tribe defeated the Romans in 410? Visigoths

249. Who was the first Mughal emperor? Babur

250. Who tutored Alexander the Great until he was 16 years old? Aristotle

Who Invented It?

1. Bifocals? Benjamin Franklin
2. E-books? Michael Hart
3. Telescope? Hans Lippershey
4. Virtual reality mounted display? Ivan Sutherland
5. Alcohol thermometer? Daniel Fahrenheit
6. Electric battery? Alessandro Volta
7. Basketball? James Naismith
8. Piano? Bartolommeo Cristofori
9. Flushing toilet? John Harrington
10. Dynamite? Alfred Nobel
11. Polio vaccine? Jonas Salk
12. Nylon? Wallace H. Carothers
13. Sewing machine? Elias Howe
14. Pacemaker? John Hoops
15. Pedal bicycle? Kirkpatrick Macmillan
16. Scotch tape? Richard Drew
17. Defibrillator? William Kouwenhoven
18. Air conditioner? Willie Carrier
19. World Wide Web? Tim Berners-Lee
20. Cotton gin? Eli Whitney
21. Blue jeans? Levi Strauss
22. Nuclear reactor? Enrico Fermi
23. Cellphone? Martin Cooper
24. Steam locomotive? Richard Trevithick

25. Chocolate chip cookies? Ruth Graves Wakefield

26. Windshield wiper? Mary Anderson

27. Piano? Bartolomeo Cristofori

28. Refrigerator? Fred Wolf

29. Pencil? Conrad Gessner

30. Paper? Cai Lun

31. Camera? Johann Zahn

32. Bionics? Jack Steele

33. Microwave oven? Percy Spencer

34. Digital camera? Steven Sasson

35. Typewriter? Christopher Latham Sholes

36. Coffee filter? Melitta Bentz

37. Spinning jenny? James Hargreaves

38. Accordion? Friedrich Buschmann

39. Electric razor? Jacob Schick

40. Traffic light? J.P. Knight

41. Horse drawn hoe? Jethro Tull

42. Lawn mower? Edwin Beard Budding

43. Brassiere? Mary Phelps Jacob

44. Corn dog? Sylvia Schur

45. Electric-powered washing machine? Alva J. Fisher

46. Zipper? Whitcomb Judson

47. Bubble gum? Walter Diemer

48. Liquid Paper? Bette Nesmith Graham

49. Telegraph? Samuel F.B. Morse

50. Frisbee? Walter Morrison

Math & Science Brainiac

1. Which planet has a white cloud pattern in its atmosphere nicknamed "Scooter"? Neptune

2. What metal melts at 30 degrees Celsius? Gallium

3. What is the strongest known natural fiber? Limpet teeth

4. What was the first element discovered through synthesis? Technetium

5. What type of gas does not undergo chemical reactions under a set of given conditions? Inert gas

6. What is the only number with the same number of letters as the meaning of its name? 4

7. Emerald and aquamarine are varieties of which gemstone? Beryl

8. What is the name of the pigment that turns leaves green? Chlorophyll

9. At what speed does light travel? 186,000 miles per second

10. What is the unit measurement for the activity of a radioactive source? Becquerel

11. What is the passage of a solvent through a semipermeable membrane from a less concentrated to a

more concentrated solution until both solutions are of the same concentration? Osmosis

12.   How many land miles are in a league? 3

13.   A Halophyte is a plant that grows in what type of solution? Saline

14.   What radioactive element is extracted from carnotite and pitchblende? Uranium

15.   How many sides does a pentadecagon have? 15

16.   What planet is the brightest natural object in the night sky? Venus

17.   How many milliliters are in 5 liters? 5,000

18.   What is the only rock that floats? Pumice

19.   What numeric scale is used to specify the acidity or basicity of an aqueous solution? pH

20.   What is the only metal that is a liquid at room temperature? Mercury

21.   What compound has a density of 1,000 kg/m³? Water

22.   What planet do the Galilean Moons orbit? Jupiter

23.   What is the cube root of 64? 4

24.   What element is combined with iron to form steel? Carbon

25.   What is the strongest known type of magnet in the universe? Magnetar

26.   How many megabytes are in one terabyte? 1,048,576

27. What metal has the highest melting point? Tungsten

28. What is a sherardized object coated with? Zinc

29. How many feet are in one mile? 5,280

30. How many times does the moon revolve around the Earth in an Earth calendar year? 13

31. How many hours are in one week? 168

32. In what year did Albert Einstein win the Nobel Prize in Physics? 1921

33. What number do the Roman numerals CCXVII equal? 109

34. How many years are in a score? 20

35. What percentage of alcohol is 70 proof whiskey? 35%

36. What instrument is used to measure atmospheric pressure? Barometer

37. How many possible ways are there to make change for a dollar? 293

38. Ethernet is a registered trademark for what company? Xerox

39. How many sides does a rhombus have? 4

40. Ascorbic acid is more commonly known as what vitamin? Vitamin C

41. What is a polygon with four unequal sides called? Quadrilateral

42. What element does every living species on Earth contain? Carbon

43. One square mile equals how many square feet? 27,878,400

44. Pascal is a measure of what? Pressure

45. What is the only planet that rotates clockwise? Venus

46. What is the name for a two-dimensional image of a slice through a three-dimensional object? Tomogram

47. The Koppen System is a classification system for what? Climate

48. What type of rock type is obsidian? Igneous

49. What term applies to space devoid of matter? Vacuum

50. How many ounces are in one ton? 32,000

51. A rainbow consists of how many colors? 7

52. The Big Dipper is a star in which constellation? Ursa Major

53. How many square miles is the total surface area of Earth? 197 million square miles

54. What is the name of a quadrilateral with two parallel sides of unequal length? Trapezium

55. What is Earth's circumference in miles? 24,901 miles

56. How many edges does a cube have? 12

57. What toxin is extracted from castor beans? Ricin

58. What is the hottest planet in the solar system? Venus

59. What type of angle measures more than 180 degrees but less than 360 degrees? Reflex angle

60. What is the most abundant protein in mammals? Collagen

61. How many feet are in one fathom? 6

62. What is the name of the bottom 9 miles of Earth's atmosphere? Troposphere

63. What element has the Periodic Table symbol He? Helium

64. How many square feet are in one acre? 43,560 square feet

65. How many inches are in 100 yards? 3,600

66. What is 531 written in Roman Numeral format? DXXXI

67. Marble is formed by the metamorphosis of what rock? Limestone

68. How many square inches are in one square foot? 144

69. How many teaspoons are in one tablespoon? 3

70. What kind of triangle has three sides with different lengths? Scalene

71. How many seconds are in a non-leap year? 31,536,000

72. How many bits are in one byte? 8

73. What is the highest prime number between 1 and 100? 97

74. How many sides does a decagon have? 10

75. What do the interior angles of a hexagon equal? 720

76. How many inches are in one mile? 63,360

77. What kind of force draws a rotating body away from the center of its rotation? Centrifugal Force

78. Dendrology is the study of what? Trees

79. How many yards are in one furlong? 220

80. What is the unit name for 1/100th of a second? Jiffy

81. What is a half of a half of a half of a half? Sixteenth

82. Nychthemeron is a period of how many consecutive hours? 24

83. How many prime numbers are between 1 to 100? 25

84. What is 1/100th of a carat weight of a gemstone called? Point

85. What is the most abundant metal in Earth's crust? Aluminum

86. What do all the numbers add up to on a standard clock face? 78

87. 1089 multiplied by 9 equals? 9801

88. What spacecraft that was launched in 1972 became the first artificial object to leave the solar system? Pioneer 10

89. How many sides does a snowflake have? 6

90. What is the name for a full moon that occurs in January? Wolf Moon

91. What is the ability of a fluid to resist flow called? Viscosity

92. What is the square root of one quarter? One half

93. How many liters are in one U.S. gallon? 3.78 liters

94. What is the world's most used man-made material? Concrete

95. How many millimeters are in one kilometer? 1,000,000

96. Which element has the highest melting point? Carbon

97. What is the square root of 225? 15

98. What is the largest moon in the solar system? Ganymede

99. What is the boiling point of water (Fahrenheit)? 212 degrees

100. Iron pyrite is commonly known as what? Fool's gold

101. What planet has the moons Phobos and Deimos? Mars

102. In physics, what is the common term for the Einstein-Rosen Bridge? Wormhole

103. What is the process of coating iron with zinc to prevent rusting called? Galvanization

104. How many planets in the solar system have rings? 4

105. At which temperature do Fahrenheit and Celsius meet? -40 degrees

106. What is measured by the SI unit called a Henry? Inductance

107. What is the eighth planet from the sun? Neptune

108. What is a positively charged ion called? Cation

109. How many stars make up Big Dipper? 7

110. Copper and zinc combined create which alloy metal? Brass

111. What does an Anemometer measure? Wind speed

112. Which is the fastest rotating planet in the solar system? Jupiter

113. Who created the Periodic Table of Elements? Dmitri Mendeleev

114. How many constellations is the night sky divided into? 88

115. How many pints are in one quart? 2

116. What unit of length is equal to approximately 3.261 light years? Parsec

117. What is the most abundant element in the air we breathe? Nitrogen

118. What was the name of the first American Space Station? Skylab

119. Which element has the Periodic Table symbol Ag? Silver

120. What color is liquid oxygen? Blue

121. How many microns are in one metric meter? 1 million

122. What is the most common element in the universe? Hydrogen

123. How many cups are in one gallon? 16

124. What does a Nephologist study? Clouds

125. How many fluid ounces are in one U.S. gallon? 128

126. One square kilometer contains how many square meters? 1 million

127. What is a single unit of quanta called? Quantum

128. What is the diameter, in millimeters, of a DVD? 120 millimeters

129. How many pixels are in one megapixel? 1,000,000

130. How many sides does a nonagon have? 9

131. How many fluid ounces are in six cups? 48

132. What is the highest number used on the pH scale? 14

133. What is the common name for nitrous oxide? Laughing Gas

134. What kind of angle is more than 90 degrees, but less than 180 degrees? Obtuse

135. How many pecks are in one bushel? 4

136. What is the most malleable metal found in nature? Gold

137. How many square inches are in one acre? 6,272,640

138. How many teaspoons are in one cup? 48

139. What is sodium hypochlorite more commonly known as? Bleach

140. How many furlongs are in one mile? 7.999 (8)

141. What is the softest mineral found in nature? Talc

142. What numbering system has a base of two? Binary

143. In what year, will Haley's Comet be visible with the naked eye from Earth? 2061

144. What is the amount of light allowed to pass through a camera lens called? Aperture

145. In vulcanization, what element is added to rubber to make it harder? Sulphur

146. What element comes last alphabetically? Zirconium

147. What is the unit of capacity for fuel wood? Cord

148. What is the chemical name for water? Dihydrogen monoxide

149. What type of eclipse occurs when Earth passes between the sun and the moon? Lunar Eclipse

150. How many yards are in one mile? 1760

151. What was the name of the first satellite sent into space? Sputnik

152. What type of substance is lignite? Coal

153. What planet is known as the Red Planet? Mars

154. What is the male part of a flower called? Stamen

155. How many centimeters are in one meter? 100

156. What is the name of the process in which ore is heated to obtain a metal? Smelting

157. What is the unit of electrical resistance? Ohm

158. What is Saturn's largest moon? Titan

159. How many carat is pure gold? 24

160. What is the densest, naturally occurring element? Osmium

161. What type of triangle has only two sides of equal length? Isosceles

162. Atomic number is the measure of what inside an atom's nucleus? Protons

163. How many times a year does the sun rise and set at the North Pole? 1

164. What unit of electrical power is equal to one joule per second? Watt

165. What was the first planet to be discovered using a telescope? Uranus

166. What is the name for the interstellar cloud of dust, hydrogen gas and plasma that is the first stage of a star's cycle? Nebula

167. What does the Saffir-Simpson Scale measure? Hurricanes

168. What is the only fundamental particle that interacts through all four of the fundamental forces? Quark

169. What is the name for the curved upper surface of a liquid in a tube? Meniscus

170. What kind of chemical bond involves the sharing of electron pairs between atoms? Covalent bond

171. How many faces does an icosahedron have? 20

172. What is the curved line between any two points on a circle called? Arc

173. At what decimal place is the 1 in 0.0001? Ten thousandths

174. What element did Pierre and Marie Curie discover in 1898? Radium

175. How many zeros does a Googol have? 100

Turn on the Television

1. What was the name of Arnold's fish on *Diff'rent Strokes*? Abraham

2. What television show character's real name is Gordon Shumway? ALF

3. Who played Barney on *How I Met Your Mother*? Neil Patrick Harris

4. What was the name of the son on *Sanford and Son*? Lamont

5. Who played Tattoo on *Fantasy Island*? Herve Villechaize

6. Who played Fire Marshall Bill on *In Living Color*? Jim Carrey

7. What was the name of Hank and Peggy Hill's son on *King of the Hill*? Bobby

8. What was the name of the son on *The Jetsons*? Elroy

9. *Lost in Space* was set in what year? 1997

10. What television show takes place in Fairplay, CO? *South Park*

11. Who played Jennifer Hart on *Hart to Hart*? Stefanie Powers

12. What was the final year of *The Tonight Show Starring Johnny Carson*? 1992

13. What was the name of Jessica Alba's character in *Dark Angel*? Max Guevara

14. Who played Hannibal Smith on *The A-Team*? George Peppard

15. On what sitcom, did Frank Sinatra make his final television appearance? Who's the Boss

16. In *House*, what is Dr. House's first name? Gregory

17. What character does Jim Parson play in *The Big Bang Theory*? Sheldon Cooper

18. What island did Balki come from on *Perfect Strangers*? Mypos

19. Who played Ari Gold in *Entourage*? Jeremy Piven

20. What was Archie Bunker's son-in-law's full name in *All in the Family*? Mike Stivic

21. Which Ingalls sister goes blind in *Little House on the Prairie*? Mary

22. On *Taxi*, what was the name of the taxi company? Sunshine Cab Company

23. Who played Major Nelson on *I Dream of Jeanie*? Larry Hagman

24. What was the mother's first name in *The Munsters*? Lily

25. What is the name of the show in which Burt Reynolds played a high school football coach? *Evening Shade*

26. How many cast members were in the first season of MTV's *The Real World*? 7

27. What is Shaggy's real name on *Scooby Doo*? Norville Rogers

28. Who played Joey Potter on *Dawson's Creek*? Katie Holmes

29. What was Maggie Simpson's first spoken word on *The Simpson's*? Daddy

30. On *Cheers*, what was Diane's last name? Chambers

31. Who plays Daryl Dixon in *The Walking Dead*? Norman Reedus

32. What was the first television series to have an African American actor in a starring role? *I Spy*

33. On *Three's Company*, what was the name of Don Knotts' character? Ralph Furley

34. How tall is Big Bird on *Sesame Street*? 8 feet 2 inches

35. What cable channel made its premiere on March 19, 1979? CSPAN

36. Who played Chief Gillespie on the television show *In the Heat of the Night*? Carroll O'Connor

37. What was the first television show filmed before a live studio audience? *I Love Lucy*

38. What was the real name of the horse, Mr. Ed? Bamboo Harvester

39. On *The Cosby Show*, how many children did Cliff and Clair Huxtable have? 5

40. Who played the daughter on *My Two Dads*? Staci Keanan

41. What cartoon character's maiden name is Betty Jean Mcbricker? Betty Rubble

42. What company had the first television commercial in 1941? Bulova watches

43. On *Mork and Mindy*, what planet is Mork from? Ork

44. What was the first animated series produced for prime-time network television? *The Flintstones*

45. Who played Tommy Solomon on *3rd Rock from the Sun*? Joseph Gordon-Levitt

46. What was the name of Priscilla Presley's character on *Dallas*? Jenna Wade

47. Who played George Costanza's father on *Seinfeld*? Jerry Stiller

48. Who played the title character in *Punky Brewster*? Soleil Moon Frye

49. What was the first name of Ross' second wife on *Friends*? Emily

50. Who played A.C. Slater on *Saved by the Bell*? Mario Lopez

51. In what year, did *Sesame Street* make its debut on PBS? 1969

52. What was the first feature length film broadcast on television? The Wizard of Oz

53. In what year were tobacco commercials banned from network television? 1971

54. What was the last name of the primary family in the television series *Bonanza*? Cartwright

55. *Saturday Night Live* made its debut in what year? 1975

56. What was the make and model of the General Lee on *Dukes of Hazard*? 1969 Dodge Charger

57. Who provided the voice of Charlie on the 1970's television show *Charlie's Angels*? John Forsythe

58. In what year did *American Bandstand* debut? 1952

59. Who played Dylan McKay on *Beverly Hills, 90210*? Luke Perry

60. What was Chandler's middle name on *Friends*? Muriel

61. What baseball team's cap did *Magnum P.I.* wear? Detroit Tigers

62. What was the name of Raymond's wife on *Everybody Loves Raymond*? Debra

63. Who played Uncle Joey on *Full House*? Dave Coulier

64. What was Topanga's maiden last name on *Boy Meets World*? Lawrence

65. Who is the youngest ever host of *Saturday Night Live*? Drew Barrymore

66. On *Three's Company*, what was Chrissy short for? Christmas

67. What was the first name of the youngest child on *Eight is Enough*? Nicholas

68. What was the first name of Leonardo DiCaprio's character on *Growing Pains*? Luke

69. Who co-starred on *Highway to Heaven* alongside Michael Landon? Victor French

70. What show was centered on the death of Laura Palmer? *Twin Pinks*

71. Who played Angela Chase on *My So-Called Life*? Claire Danes

72. What television show featured one of the co-stars owning a Coyote X car? Hardcastle and McCormick

73. Who played Kap'n Karl on *Pee-wee's Playhouse*? Phil Hartman

74. On what show, did Yogi Bear make his debut? The Huckleberry Hound Show

75. What television series was set in the year 2258? Babylon 5

76. What fictional college was used as the setting for *A Different World*? Hillman College

77. In what year did the original *Star Trek* television series make its debut? 1966

78. Who played Lauren Miller on *Family Ties*? Courtney Cox

79. What television show featured the characters Jennifer Marlowe, Herb Tarlek, and Les Nessman? WKRP in Cincinnati

80. What was the butler's name on *Fresh Prince of Bel-Air*? Geoffrey

81. Who played Peter Brady on *The Brady Bunch*? Christopher Knight

82. In what year, did Bob Barker make his debut as host of *The Price is Right*? 1972

83. What was the name of the Connor's son on *Roseanne*? D.J.

84. What was Fran's last name on *The Nanny*? Fine

85. On *Frasier*, what was the name of Martin Crane's dog? Eddie

86. In *I Love Lucy*, who played Ethel Mertz? Vivian Vance

87. What is the first name of the adopted father of Alvin, Simon and Theodore? Dave

88. What was the name of the detective agency on *Moonlighting*? Blue Moon

89. Which Teenage Mutant Ninja Turtle wears orange? Michelangelo

90. Who played The Siren in the original *Batman* series? Joan Collins

91. Who was the first host of *Family Feud*? Richard Dawson

92. Who played Colonel Steve Austin on *The Six Million Dollar Man*? Lee Majors

93. What city was the setting for *One Day at a Time*? Indianapolis, IN

94. What variety show featured Minnie Pearl, Buck Owens and Junior Samples? Hee-Haw

95. What was the name of Mr. Kotter's wife on *Welcome Back, Kotter*? Julie

96. What 1980's television show featured a pilot named Stringfellow Hawke? Airwolf

97. In what year did the *Mickey Mouse Club* make its debut? 1955

98. What was the first name of David Hasselhoff's character on *Baywatch*? Mitch

99. On *Happy Days*, what was Warren Weber's nickname? Potsie

100. For what show, did John Larroquette earn three consecutive Emmy Awards for Supporting Actor? Night Court

101. What cartoon is set in Frostbite Falls, MN? *Rocky and Bullwinkle*

102. What was the name of Alan's son on *Two and a Half Men*? Jake

103. Who played Tom Hanson on *21 Jump Street*? Johnny Depp

104. What was the name of Matt Dillon's horse on *Gunsmoke*? Buck

105. What television show was set aboard *The Pacific Princess*? The Love Boat

106. What was Kevin's last name on *The Wonder Years*? Arnold

107. Greg and Kim Warner were married characters on what television show? Yes, Dear

108. Who played Detective Sipowicz on *NYPD Blue*? Dennis Franz

109. What city was the setting for *The Wire*? Baltimore, MD

110. Evan Marriott was the subject of what reality television show? Joe Millionaire

111. Mark, Randy and Brad were the couple's children on what sitcom? *Home Improvement*

112. What was Buffy's last name on *Buffy the Vampire Slayer*? Summers

113. What show featured Sergeant Bilko? The Phil Silvers Show

114. What is the most money a contestant can possibly win on a single episode of *Jeopardy!*? $566,400

115. What was Hawkeye's first name on *MASH*? Benjamin

116. In what city did *Matlock* take place? Atlanta, GA

117. What was Charlotte's last name on *Sex and the City*? York

118. Who played Carrie Heffernan on *The King of Queens*? Leah Remini

119. What was the name of Tony and Carmela's daughter on *The Soprano's*? Meadow

120. What was the last name of Bryan Cranston's character on *Breaking Bad*? White

121. On what television show, did Helen Hunt play Jamie Buchman? *Mad About You*

122. What was Dharma's maiden name on, *Dharma & Greg*? Finkelstein

123. In what year, did *Law & Order* debut? 1990

124. What was the first name of the George and Louise's son on *The Jeffersons*? Lionel

125. What was Opie's last name on *The Andy Griffith Show*? Taylor

Take Me to the Zoo

1. What is the world's largest cat? Siberian Tiger
2. What insect is responsible for transmitting the Bubonic Plague? Flea
3. What is the world's largest bird of prey? Condor
4. How many legs does a lobster have? 10
5. What is a male ferret called? Hob
6. What is the deadliest spider on Earth? Brazilian Wandering Spider
7. Pan Troglodytes is the scientific name for what animal? Chimpanzee
8. What is the only bird with nostrils at the end of its beak? Kiwi
9. What delicacy comes from the roe of wild sturgeon? Caviar
10. How many legs does a scorpion have? 8
11. What type of acid is secreted by red ants and stinging nettles? Formic acid
12. Other than humans, what is the only primate capable of having blue eyes? Black Lemur
13. What color is yak milk? Pink
14. How many noses does a slug have? 4

15. A black panther is what kind of big cat? Leopard
16. How many hearts does an octopus have? 3
17. What kind of animal is a geoduck? Clam
18. Which is the world's fastest moving land snake? Black Mamba
19. What type of animal lives in a holt? Otter
20. What is the most common mammal in the U.S.? Mouse
21. The pudu is the world's smallest species of what animal? Deer
22. How many legs do butterflies have? 6
23. What is a female alligator called? Tresor
24. What is the only bird from which leather can be obtained? Ostrich
25. What type of animal is a saluki? Dog
26. What is the world's largest reptile? Saltwater Crocodile
27. What type of insect lives in a formicarium? Ant
28. What is the largest member of the deer family? Moose
29. What is a female skunk called? Sow
30. How many teeth does an African elephant have? 4
31. What is the world's slowest moving vertebrate animal on land? Three-toed sloth
32. What is the only mammal able to fly? Bat
33. What is a pregnant goldfish called? Twit
34. What color is a lobster's blood? Blue

35. Animals that eat both plants and animals are called what? Omnivore

36. What is the cross between a donkey and a zebra called? Zedonk

37. What is the world's largest rodent? Capybara

38. What bird has Golden and Argus varieties? Pheasant

39. What is a group of rhinoceroses called? Crash

40. What is the only mammal that sleeps on its back? Human

41. What is stored in a camel's hump? Fat

42. What animal has the highest known blood pressure of any mammal in the world? Giraffe

43. How many legs does a ladybug (ladybird) have? 6

44. What type of animal is an echidna? Anteater

45. Besides humans, what is the only other mammal with a chin? Elephant

46. What is the largest animal Earth has ever seen? Blue Whale

47. What is another name for a warrigal? Dingo

48. What is the only breed of dog that can get gout? Dalmatian

49. How many total whiskers does a cat have? 24

50. What type of fish is a sockeye? Salmon

51. What is a beaver's home called? Lodge

52. What is the only bird that can fly backwards? Hummingbird

53. What type of animal is a sitatunga? Antelope

54. What mammal uses echolocation? Bat

55. What is a camel with two humps called? Bactrian

56. What type of fish is a skipjack? Tuna

57. How many days is the gestation period of a kangaroo? 33

58. What is a baby oyster called? Spat

59. What does a lepidopterist study? Butterflies

60. What is the name for a whale's penis? Dork

61. What is the world's shortest mammal? Bumblebee bat

62. What is the only marsupial native to North America? Opossum

63. What is the world's loudest insect? Male cicada

64. What type of bird is a pochard? Duck

65. What does a carpophagus animal feed on? Fruit

66. How many nipples does a dog have? 10

67. The ratel is more commonly known by what name? Honey Badger

68. What is helminthology the study of? Worms

69. What is the world's largest beetle? Goliath beetle

70. What does an ungulate animal have? Hoofs

71. How many legs does a queen bee have? 6

72. What is the only animal that can see both infra-red and ultra-violet light? Goldfish

73. What is the only bird that has two penises? Swan

74. Alurpoda Melanoleuca is the scientific name for what animal? Panda bear

75. What breed of dog is a Blenheim? Spaniel

76. What animal has the world's largest eyes? Giant squid

77. What is the name for a group of kangaroos? Mob

78. What is the world's largest freshwater turtle? Alligator Snapping Turtle

79. What is a baby giraffe called? Calf

80. What is the name for a tiger's paw prints? Pug marks

81. What is the only cat on Earth that can't retract its claws? Cheetah

82. Trakehner and Irish Draught are both breeds of what animal? Horse

83. What is the world's largest amphibian? Giant Salamander

84. What are a cat's whiskers called? Vibrissae

85. Lanner and Merlin are both types of what bird? Falcon

86. What is the world's subspecies of brown bear? Kodiak

87. What is the national animal of Canada? Beaver

88. Macaroni, Gentoo and Chinstrap are all types of what bird? Penguins

89. What is the only insect that can turn its head? Praying Mantis

90. What insect is a Pullicologist an expert on? Flea

91. What is the name for a baby beaver? Kitten

92. How many teeth does a mosquito have? 47

93. What is the world's largest monkey? Mandrill

94. What is a group of owls called? Parliament

95. What is a gruntle? Pig's snout

96. The Rhodesian Ridgeback dog was originally bred to hunt what cat? Lion

97. What type of animal is a pinniped? Seal

98. What is the world's fastest two-legged animal? Ostrich

99. What is a female fox called? Vixen

100. What is the name of the sticky wax obtained from sheep? Lanolin

101. What extinct bird was native to the island of Mauritius? Dodo

102. What is the world's largest marsupial? Kangaroo

103. What dog breed was originally bred to hunt badgers? Dachshunds

104. What kind of animal is a Terrapin? Turtle

105. What is the largest lizard native to North America? Green Lizard

106. How many chromosomes does a goldfish have? 94

107. What is the world's largest crab? Japanese Spider Crab

108. What type of mammal has rectangular pupils? Goat

109. What animal lays the world's largest egg? Whale shark

110. What is the only breed of dog that doesn't have a pink tongue? Chow

111. How many chambers does an elk's stomach have? 4

112. What type of mammal is a Flying Fox? Bat

113. By weight, what is the world's largest snake? Anaconda

114. In what country did the Basset Hound originate? France

115. What type of insect is a Purple Emperor? Butterfly

116. What is the world's largest mollusk? Giant Clam

117. What is a female donkey called? Jenny

118. How many eyes does a scallop have? 35

119. What rodent has the longest gestation period? Porcupine

120. Nurse, Carpet and Wobbegong are all examples of what type of fish? Shark

121. Which of its body parts does a butterfly use for taste? Feet

122. What is the largest breed of domesticated cat? Maine Coon

123. What type of animal is nicknamed the River Horse? Hippopotamus

124. What type of animal is a Blue-Footed Booby? Bird

125. What is the only animal born with horns? Giraffe

Music is My Life

1. How many Grammy Awards has Elvis Presley won? 3

2. At what age did Janis Joplin, Jimi Hendrix and Kurt Cobain all die at? 27

3. Where did Puff the Magic Dragon live? Hanalei

4. What band released the single, "Eternal Flame" in 1989? The Bangles

5. Who was the last act at Woodstock? Jimi Hendrix

6. What song by The Rolling Stones was a tribute to David Bowie's ex-wife? "Angie"

7. What band was named after a scientist from the movie *Barbarella*? Duran Duran

8. Who was the first person to appear on the cover of *Rolling Stone* magazine? John Lennon

9. What hymn was written by John Newton in 1748? "Amazing Grace"

10. Who is the only member of The Rolling Stones to have a number one hit as a solo artist? Bill Wyman

11. Which album by Wings includes "Picasso's Last Words"? Band on the Run

12. Which orchestral instrument can play the highest note? Violin

13.   What lead singer was born Farrokh Bulsara? Freddie Mercury

14.   What was the first name of Ritchie Valens' high school sweetheart whom he wrote a song for? Donna

15.   What is the all-time bestselling movie soundtrack? The Bodyguard: Original Soundtrack Album

16.   What is a plectrum? Guitar pick

17.   What musical group had the 1967 Top 10 single, "I Think We're Alone Now"? Tommy James and the Shondells

18.   What was the most played song on American radio during the 20th century? "You've Lost That Loving Feeling"

19.   Who is the oldest member of the Spice Girls? Geri Halliwell

20.   Who was musical director of the New York Philharmonic from 1958 to 1970? Leonard Bernstein

21.   In 2008, who won the Grammy Award for Best New Artist? Amy Winehouse

22.   What famous hymn did Julia Ward Howe write in 1861? "Battle Hymn of the Republic"

23.   Who is the lead singer of Evanescence? Amy Lee

24.   Who had the first country music album to top the U.S. Pop Album charts? Johnny Cash

25.   Who wrote the musical composition "Rhapsody in Blue"? George Gershwin

26. What composer is known as the Father of the String Quartet? Joseph Haydn

27. "The Dance" and "Rodeo" were released by what country music singer? Garth Brooks

28. What former Victoria Secret model appeared in the Guns N' Roses videos "Don't Cry" and "November Rain"? Stephanie Seymour

29. What is the minimum number of musicians a band must have to be considered a Big Band? 10

30. Bjork was lead singer of what Icelandic band before pursuing a solo career? The Sugarcubes

31. What singer released an album in 1984, called *Alf*? Alison Moyet

32. Who did Mariah Carey marry on June 5, 1993? Tommy Mottola

33. How many strings are on a ukulele? 4

34. Who was the first hispanic to be inducted into the Rock and Roll Hall of Fame? Carlos Santana

35. What band had the 1979 #1 single, "My Sharona"? The Knack

36. What guitarist is known as Slowhand? Eric Clapton

37. Who replaced Ozzy Osbourne as Black Sabbath's lead singer in 1979? Ronnie James Dio

38. What is a Marimba? Bass xylophone

39. Who did The Mothers of Invention back up? Frank Zappa

40. Who was the oldest member of The Jackson 5? Jackie Jackson

41. What band released the album, *Thirty Seconds Over Winterland*? Jefferson Airplane

42. What instrument is the playing style Clawhammer associated with? Banjo

43. What band released the 1990 single, "Groove is in the Heart"? Deee-Lite

44. What is the largest brass section instrument in an orchestra? Tuba

45. In what city was the first American commercial radio station located? Pittsburgh, PA

46. What was the name of the first pop music video released in 1975? "Bohemian Rhapsody"

47. Which blues great was born Ellas Otha Bates? Bo Diddley

48. What note does an orchestra tune to? A

49. What singer released the 1978 album, *Here, My Dear*? Marvin Gaye

50. Robert Alan Zimmerman is the birth name of what singer? Bob Dylan

51. What is the title of Beethoven's only opera? "Fidelio"

52. Who had the #1 song, "The Battle of New Orleans"? Johnny Horton

53. How many keys does a grand piano have? 88

54. Who is the only person inducted twice into the Country Music Hall of Fame? Roy Rogers

55. How old was Mozart when he wrote, "Twinkle, Twinkle, Little Star"? 5

56. Who was the first artist signed to The Beatles' Apple Records label? James Taylor

57. Chaim Witz is the real name of what musician? Gene Simmons

58. Who composed "The Ride of the Valkyries"? Richard Wagner

59. What band had the 1983 hit song, "Too Shy"? Kajagoogoo

60. The Eagles were formerly the backing group for what singer? hLinda Rondstadt

61. Stanley Burrell became famous as which recording artist? MC Hammer

62. In what year was the single, "We Are the World" released? 1985

63. What was the second video to air on MTV? "You Better Run" by Pat Benetar

64. Identical twins Charlie and Craig Reid had what Top 10 song in 1993? "I'm Gonna Be" (500 Miles)

65. What is the name of the Steve Winwood fronted band that was inducted into the Rock and Roll Hall of Fame in 2004? Traffic

66. What rapper's real name is Marshall Mathers? Eminem

67. How many notes comprise a musical scale? 8

68. Yo-Yo Ma has won Grammy Awards for playing which musical instrument? Cello

69. What jazz musician released the album *Blue Train* in 1957? John Coltrane

70. What band did Stevie Ray Vaughn co-found in 1978? Double Trouble

71. What artist won the Grammy Award for Album of the Year for *Nick of Time*? Bonnie Raitt

72. Who released the song "Stand by Me" in 1961? Ben E. King

73. Who was lead singer of AC/DC before his death in 1980? Bon Scott

74. Mel Schacher, Mark Farner and Don Brewer were founding members of what rock band? Grand Funk Railroad

75. Syd Barrett was a founding member of which Rock and Roll Hall of Fame rock band? Pink Floyd

76. Who did Van Halen guitarist Eddie Van Halen marry in 1981? Valerie Bertinelli

77. Ian Curtis was lead singer of which rock group before he committed suicide in 1980? Joy Division

78. What rock band released the songs "Limelight" and "Vital Signs"? Rush

79. What singer had the 1987 #1 single, "I Think We're Alone Now"? Tiffany

80. What is the density and level of music measured in? Decibels

81. Who was lead singer of Def Leppard when they released *Hysteria*? Joe Elliott

82. Who was the first Country Music Association (CMA) Entertainer of the Year? Eddy Arnold

83. In 1978, what musician was charged with killing Nancy Spungen? Sid Vicious

84. What 1960's rock band was Peter Noone a vocalist for? Herman's Hermits

85. Who composed "Minute Waltz"? Frederic Chopin

86. What band released the album *The Gilded Palace of Sin*? The Flying Burrito Brothers

87. What group was Bobby Brown a member of before pursuing a solo career? New Edition

88. What was Aerosmith's first #1 song? "I Don't Want to Miss a Thing"

89. What top alternative rock group was founded in 1987, in Aberdeen, WA? Nirvana

90. Who was the first female inducted into the Rock & Roll Hall of Fame? Aretha Franklin

91. Who wrote the score for "The Nutcracker"? Tchaikovsky

92. In 1961, who released the song "Runaround Sue"? Dion

93. Who was the first rock group to use lasers in a live performance? The Who

94. What name is guitarist Saul Hudson more commonly known by? Slash

95. "Load up on guns, bring your friends," is the opening line of what famous alternative rock song? "Smells Like Teen Spirit"

96. How old was George Harrison when he joined The Beatles? 14

97. What British band released the song, "Another Brick on the Wall"? Pink Floyd

98. What is the last note on a standard keyboard? C

99. Who wrote both "St John Passion" and "St Mark Passion"? Johan Sebastian Bach

100. *Coal Miner's Daughter* is a film based on the life of what female singer? Loretta Lynn

101. What singer had the 1955 hit song "Blue Suede Shoes"? Carl Perkins

102. What rapper's real name is O'Shea Jackson? Ice Cube

103. Who was lead singer of The Smiths? Morrissey

104. In what country was the band INXS founded? Australia

105. What was Diana Ross' first solo #1 single? "Ain't No Mountain High Enough"

106. Who was lead singer of Journey when they released *Escape*? Steve Perry

107. "Smoke on the Water" was originally released on which Deep Purple album? *Machine Head*

108. What band's name is based on the last name pseudonym used by Paul McCartney? Ramones

109. Chris Cornell, Jeff Ament and Eddie Vedder were all members of what alternative rock band? Temple of the Dog

110. What singer has the top selling country music album of all-time? Shania Twain

111. In what year, did ABBA form? 1972

112. As a member of what band was Eric Clapton first inducted into the Rock and Roll Hall of Fame? The Yardbirds

113. "There's a lady who's sure all that glitters is gold" is the opening line to what song? "Stairway to Heaven"

114. What rock band featured Rikki Rockett, C.C. DeVille and Bobby Dall? Poison

115. Who composed "La fanciulla del West"? Giacomo Puccini

116. How old was Hank Williams when he died in 1953? 29

117. Who was lead singer of Big Brother and the Holding Company? Janis Joplin

118. In what year did The Eagles release *Hotel California*? 1976

119. What band are Danny Wood, Jordan Knight and Joey McIntyre all members of? New Kids on the Block

120. Who was the first person to be inducted twice into the Rock and Roll Hall of Fame? Clyde McPhatter

121. Who released *Miracles: The Holiday Album*? Kenny G

122. What song holds the record for being #1 on the Billboard Hot 100 for sixteen straight weeks? "One Sweet Day"

123. Who conducted the scores for the three original *Star Wars* movies? John Williams

124. Who released the 1991 song, "I'm Too Sexy"? Right Said Fred

125. Madonna's song "Crazy for You" was originally released on what movie's soundtrack? *Vision Quest*

Movie Extraordinaire

1. Who directed *Gone with the Wind*? Victor Fleming

2. What is Red's first name in *Shawshank Redemption*? Ellis

3. In *Back to the Future*, what did the DeLorean's license plate say? OUTATIME

4. In what movie, did Ethan Hawke make his film debut? *Explorers*

5. What 1993 film starred Ben Affleck, Jason London and Parker Posey? *Dazed and Confused*

6. Who played Jennifer Cavalleri in the 1970 film, *Love Story*? Ali McGraw

7. Who played Diane Court in, *Say Anything*? Ione Skye

8. What is Gedde Watanabe's character's name in *Sixteen Candles*? Long Duk Dong

9. What was the real name of the killer whale in *Free Willy*? Keiko

10. Who played Annette Hargrove in *Cruel Intentions*? Reese Witherspoon

11. How many actors have played "007" in the *James Bond* movies? 6

12. What is Dorothy's last name in *The Wizard of Oz*? Gale

13. What actor was the biggest box-office draw during the 1980's? Harrison Ford

14. Who was the first African American to win two Academy Awards for acting? Denzel Washington

15. Who played Mick Dundee in *Crocodile Dundee*? Paul Hogan

16. In *Officer and a Gentleman*, which character commits suicide? Sid Worley

17. What is the name of the first James Bond film? *Dr. No*

18. In what film does the cast prepare for Rex Manning Day? *Empire Records*

19. What is Lt. Dan's last name in *Forrest Gump*? Taylor

20. In *Dumb and Dumber*, what is the name of Harry's pet bird? Petey

21. What was the name of Ray Liotta's character in *Goodfellas*? Henry Hill

22. *The Blind Side* is based on the life of what NFL player? Michael Oher

23. In *Beetlejuice*, what is Adam and Barbara's last name? Maitland

24. Jock, Pedro and Trusty are all characters in which Disney film? *Lady and the Tramp*

25. Who received the first posthumous Academy Award nomination? James Dean

26. In *Short Circuit*, what was the name of the talking robot? Number Five

27. In what film does Robert De Niro play a gangster named Noodles? *Once Upon a Time in America*

28. What Francis Ford Coppola film was based on the novel, *The Heart of Darkness*? *Apocalypse Now*

29. In what year does *Dirty Dancing* take place? 1963

30. In *Pulp Fiction*, what was Vincent's last name? Vega

31. What is Jim's last name in *American Pie*? Levenstein

32. Who directed *Lost in Translation*? Sofia Coppola

33. What is the name of Matt Dillon's band in *Singles*? Citizen Dick

34. In *Juno*, who gets Juno pregnant? Bleeker

35. Who played Howard Hughes in *The Aviator*? Leonardo DiCaprio

36. What is the name of the hotel *in The Shining*? Overlook Hotel

37. How many films are in the *Harry Potter* series? 8

38. In *Star Wars*, what is R2D2 shorthand for? Reel 2, Dialogue 2

39. Who played John Shaft in the 2000 remake of *Shaft*? Samuel L. Jackson

40. What is the name of the prospector in *Toy Story 2*? Stinky Pete

41. What was the first movie to earn $100,000,000 at the box office? *Jaws*

42. Who played Brian in *The Breakfast Club*? Anthony Michael Hall

43. In what film did Clint Eastwood first play "The Man with No Name"? *A Fistful of Dollars*

44. Who directed *Backdraft*? Ron Howard

45. What is the name of the high school John Travolta and Olivia Newton John attend in *Grease*? Rydell High

46. What 1983 film did Barbra Streisand direct? *Yentl*

47. What was the name of the FBI agent Jodie Foster played in *Silence of the Lambs*? Clarice Starling

48. What was the first film to be nominated for Academy Awards for both Best Foreign Language Film and Best Picture? *Z*

49. In *Top Gun*, what is the name of the aircraft carrier Maverick and Goose are stationed aboard? USS *Enterprise*

50. Who wrote the screenplay for *Sense and Sensibility*? Emma Thompson

51. What is the name of the barn cat in *101 Dalmatians*? Sergeant Tibbs

52. In what film does Marlon Brando play the character Terry Malloy? *On the Waterfront*

53. What was the first G-rated film to win the Academy Award for Best Picture? *Oliver!*

54. Who was the first African American to win an Academy Award? Hattie McDaniel

55. Who played Jake Gittes in *Chinatown*? Jack Nicholson

56. What was Adam Sandler's occupation in *Big Daddy*? Tollbooth Worker

57. What film director's real name is Allen Stewart Konigsberg? Woody Allen

58. What film won the 1990 Academy Award for Best Picture? *Dances with Wolves*

59. In what 1984 film was Elisabeth Shue's character named Ali Mills? *The Karate Kid*

60. In what movie, did Johnny Depp make his debut film appearance? *A Nightmare on Elm Street*

61. Who played Mr. Pink in *Reservoir Dogs*? Steve Buscemi

62. What was the first film to win the Academy Award for Best Animated Feature? Shrek

63. Who played Vin in the original, *The Magnificent Seven*? Steve McQueen

64. What was the first PG rated Pixar movie? The Incredibles

65. Who played Danny Ocean in the 1960 film *Ocean's Eleven*? Frank Sinatra

66. In December 2007, the Empire State Building in New York was illuminated yellow to promote what film? The Simpsons Movie

67. Who directed *Platoon*? Oliver Stone

68. What was the name of the spaceship in *ALIEN*? Nostromo

69. What was the first animated film nominated for the Academy Award as Best Picture? Beauty and the Beast

70. Who directed *Full Metal Jacket*? Stanley Kubrick

71. What was the name of James Deans' character in *Rebel Without a Cause*? Jim Stark

72. What 2008 film is set on the fictional Greek island Kalokairi? Mamma Mia

73. What was the first movie with stereo sound? Fantasia

74. Who played Roman in *The Great Outdoors*? Dan Akroyd

75. Who was the first female director to have a film earn over $100 million at the box office? Penny Marshall

76. What actor was born Issur Danielovitch Demsky? Kirk Douglas

77. What was the first John Grisham novel to be made into a movie? *The Firm*

78. What is the name of the giant bird in *UP*? Kevin

79. What was the name of the orangutan in *Every Which Way but Loose*? Clyde

80. Who directed *Clerks* and *Chasing Amy*? Kevin Smith

81. Who played Dark Helmet in *Spaceballs*? Rick Moranis

82. What was the first PG-13 rated film released in the United States? Red Dawn (1984)

83. Who did the voice of Diego in *Ice Age*? Dennis Leary

84. What was the first movie that Goldie Hawn and Kurt Russell co-stared in together? Overboard

85. What is the name of the college in *National Lampoon's Animal House*? Faber College

86. What was the first musical to win the Academy Award for Best Picture? The Broadway Melody

87. What was the name of Nemo's father in *Finding Nemo*? Marlin

88. In which James Bond film did Jane Seymour play Solitaire? Live and Let Die

89. Who is the youngest person to ever win an Academy Award? Tatum O'Neal

90. What animal inspired the title character in *King Kong*? Komodo dragon

91. What was the name of Ariel's crab friend in *The Little Mermaid*? Sebastian

92. Who played Brad Majors in *The Rocky Horror Picture Show*? Barry Bostwick

93. In *Star Trek*, what is Captain Kirk's middle name? Tiberius

94. Who has won the most Academy Awards? Walt Disney

95. What was the last movie released on VHS? *A History of Violence*

96. Who directed *The Sixth Sense*? M. Night Shyamalan

97. Who played Bud Fox in *Wall Street*? Charlie Sheen

98. What was Tom Cruise's first movie? *Endless Love*

99. Who played Shoeless Joe Jackson in *Field of Dreams*? Ray Liotta

100. What was the name of the Good Witch of the North in *The Wizard of Oz*? Glinda

101. Who won an Academy Award for his portrayal of Ray Charles in the *Ray*? Jamie Foxx

102. What actor died during the filming of *The Crow*? Brandon Lee

103. Which is the only one of Disney's seven dwarfs who does not have a beard? Dopey

104. Who won the Academy Award for Best Actress for her portrayal of Marilyn Monroe in *My Weekend with Marilyn*? Michelle Williams

105. What was the last movie released on laserdisc? *End of Days*

106. In *Shaun of the Dead*, what is the name of Shaun's girlfriend? Liz

107. Before Tom Hanks accepted the role, who turned down the part of Woody in *Toy Story*? Billy Crystal

108. What city is the setting for *Robocop*? Detroit

109. What movie was the last film appearance for both Marilyn Monroe and Clarke Gable? The Misfits

110. What movie holds the record for earning the most money at the box office without ever being #1 at the box office? My Big Fat Greek Wedding

111. In *Pretty Woman*, what make of car is Edward driving when he first picks up Vivian? Lotus

112. In *Splash*, what is the name of the female mermaid? Madison

113. In *Lady and the Tramp*, what is the aunt's name? Sarah

114. In *Napoleon Dynamite*, who is Napoleon playing tetherball with at the end of the film? Deb

115. What is the name of the Nobel Laureate character that Russell Crowe played in *A Beautiful Mind*? John Forbes Nash, Jr.

116. Who was the first African American to receive an Academy Award nomination for Best Actress and Best Supporting Actress? Whoopi Goldberg

117. What actress' real name is Edda van Heemstra? Audrey Hepburn

118. In *Titanic*, what is Jack's last name? Dawson

119. Who did the voice of Gru in *Despicable Me*? Steve Carell

120. How old was Laurence Fishburne when he got his role as a Navy Gunners Mate in *Apocalypse Now*? 14

121. What was Shirley Temple's first film? The Red-Haired Alibi

122. In what year were movies first released on VHS? 1977

123. For what movie, did Steven Spielberg win his first Academy Award for Best Director? Schindler's List

124. Who played Trapper John in *MASH* (movie)? Elliott Gould

125. What is the name of the hockey team that Paul Newman plays for in *Slap Shot*? Charleston Chiefs

Around the World in Sports

1. Who was the first African American to win the Heisman Trophy? Ernie Davis

2. Who holds the record for the most saves in a Major League season? Francisco Rodgriguez

3. Who was the first gymnast to score a perfect 10 score? Nadia Comaneci

4. Where did Roger Staubach play college football? U.S. Naval Academy

5. Who was the #1 overall pick in the 1989 NBA draft? Pervis Ellison

6. How many Super Bowls have the Pittsburgh Steelers played in? 8

7. How many of golf's majors did Jack Nicklaus win? 18

8. How many games long is Joe DiMaggio's consecutive hits streak? 56

9. Who hit the "Homer in the Gloamin" on September 28, 1938? Gabby Hartnett

10. What is the largest U.S. state capital without a professional sports franchise? Austin

11. How many strikes are needed to record a 300 in ten pin bowling? 12

12. On a standard dartboard, what number lies between 12 and 20? 5

13. In what year was the first Kentucky Derby run? 1875

14. What is the playing surface for The French Open tennis tournament? Clay

15. Tice and Pioneer are terms used in which game? Croquet

16. How many lanes does an Olympic swimming pool have? 8

17. In what year did the Cleveland Indians last win the World Series? 1948

18. Who was the first unseeded tennis player to win the Wimbledon Men's Final? Boris Becker

19. Who was the only club to win two World Series' in the 1980's? LA Dodgers

20. In what sport, would you use a dagger and a trapeze? Sailing

21. What was the first NFL team to put a logo on their helmets? Los Angeles Rams

22. Santos and Corinthians are both professional soccer clubs in what country? Brazil

23. Steve Prefontaine ran track for what university? University of Oregon

24. How many feet wide is a regulation NFL football field? 160 feet

25. In what year did the United States Football League (USFL) disband? 1987

26. Who was the last player to win the MLB Triple Crown? Miguel Cabrera

27. In what year did the first Ryder Cup take place? 1927

28. Who is the only world heavyweight boxing champion to finish his career without ever having been defeated? Rocky Marciano

29. Who was on the cover of the first *Sports Illustrated*? Eddie Matthews

30. What was Babe Ruth's first name? George

31. Who was the first high school player to be drafted #1 overall in the NBA Draft? Kwame Brown

32. In what year did the Brooklyn Dodgers win their only World Series? 1955

33. In what country was, "The Rumble in the Jungle" fought? Zaire

34. How many quarterbacks were taken in the first round of the 2011 NFL draft? 4

35. In 1964, what Baltimore Colts running back became the first NFL player to score 20 touchdowns in a regular season? Lenny Moore

36. What Kansas City Chiefs player set the NFL record with seven sacks in a 1990 game against the Seattle Seahawks? Derrick Thomas

37. What country will host the 2022 FIFA World Cup? Qatar

38. In 1924, the first Winter Olympics were held in what country? France

39. Who was the last MLB pitcher to throw over 300 innings in a single season? Steve Carlton

40. How many Heisman Trophy winners have been from Notre Dame? 7

41. Who was head coach of the 1992 men's Olympic basketball team? Chuck Daly

42. What male tennis player reached the final of every U.S. Open between 1982 and 1989? Ivan Lendl

43. Who was the first MLB player to win a batting title in three different decades? George Brett

44. In 1958, who became the youngest footballer, at age 17, to play in the FIFA World Cup? Pele

45. Who holds the record for the most rushing yards in a Super Bowl game? Timmy Smith

46. How many feet wide is a regulation volleyball court? 30 feet

47. How many NCAA basketball championships did John Wooden win while head coach of UCLA? 10

48. Who was the last MLB pitcher to win 300 games? Randy Johnson

49. Who was the first player to break the NHL single season 100-point mark? Phil Esposito

50. Andre Agassi's father represented what country in boxing at the 1948 and 1952 Olympics? Iran

51. Who was the first South American to win The Masters? Angel Cabrera

52. In what year, did Jackie Robinson make his debut with the Brooklyn Dodgers? 1947

53. Which NFL team drafted John Elway? Baltimore Colts

54. Who did the USA hockey team defeat after the USSR to win the gold medal at the 1980 Winter Olympics? Finland

55. What country has won the most medals at the Olympic Winter games? Norway

56. What is the largest participant sport in the world? Fishing

57. Who was the first American to win the Tour de France? Greg LeMond

58. Where did Mia Hamm play collegiate soccer? University of North Carolina

59. Who founded the Special Olympics in 1968? Eunice Kennedy Shriver

60. Who was the last Major League pitcher to win 30 or more games in a season? Denny McLain

61. Which NFL team drafted actor Burt Reynolds? Baltimore Colts

62. In what year was the first MLB game televised? 1939

63. In what sport, does Herve Filion hold the record with 14,084 wins? Harness Racing

64. Who holds the NBA record for the most career fouls? Kareem Abdul-Jabbar

65. How many Daytona 500 races did Dale Earnhardt Sr. win? One

66. For what team did Nolan Ryan pitch in his only World Series? New York Mets

67. How many stitches are on an official Major League baseball? 108 double stitches

68. Who holds the record for the most PGA Tour wins? Sam Snead

69. Who was the first sophomore to win the Heisman Trophy? Tim Tebow

70. What award is given to the MVP of the NHL's Stanley Cup Playoffs? Conn Smythe Trophy

71. In what sport did Ronda Rousey win an Olympic bronze medal? Judo

72. At how many different positions was Pete Rose a MLB All-Star? 5

73. Who was second to Tiger Woods at the 1997 Masters Championship? Tom Kite

74. Who is the only MLB player to hit 60 or more home runs in three different seasons? Sammy Sosa

75. What team holds the NBA record for most consecutive losses? Cleveland Cavaliers

76. The first FIFA World Cup was held in what country in 1930? Uruguay

77. For what sport is The Iroquois Cup awarded? Lacrosse

78. Where did Pete Maravich play college basketball? Louisiana State University

79. Who was the first athlete depicted on a Wheaties box? Lou Gehrig (1934)

80. What college football team won the first BCS Championship? University of Tennessee

81. What is the only U.S. city in which all the major sports teams wear the same colors? Pittsburgh, PA

82. Who is the only player to be named Super Bowl MVP from the losing team? Chuck Howley

83. Who holds the MLB record for the most hits in a single season? Ichiro Suzuki

84. Who is the only American born driver to win the Formula One World Drivers' Championship? Phil Hill

85. Who was the first person to run a mile in under four minutes? Roger Bannister

86. Who won the gold medal in Men's Figure Skating at the 1988 Winter Olympics? Brian Boitano

87. How many games long is Cal Ripken Jr.'s consecutive games played streak? 2,632

88. Who is the WNBA all-time leader in points scored? Tina Thompson

89. What was the last horse to win horse racing's Triple Crown? American Pharoah

90. Who did Mike Tyson defeat in 1986 to become WBC Heavyweight champion? Trevor Berbick

91. Who holds the MLB record for the most wins by a left-handed pitcher? Warren Spahn

92. Whose image is used in the NBA logo? Jerry West

93. What NFL team won the most games during the 1970's? Dallas Cowboys

94. How many free throws did Shaquille O'Neal miss during his entire NBA career? 5,317

95. In what year were women first allowed to participate in the Olympic Games? 1900

96. Where is the Negro League Baseball Hall of Fame located? Kansas City, Missouri

97. Who was the first player to win an NCAA basketball championship, Olympic gold medal, and NBA Championship? Clyde Lovellette

98. What minor league baseball team did Michael Jordan play for? Birmingham Barons

99. Who won the first NBA Slam Dunk Contest in 1984? Larry Nance

100. What was the first NHL team to win five consecutive Stanley Cups? Montreal Canadians

101. Who was the first African American ever selected in the NBA draft? Chuck Cooper

102. Who is the only two-time winner of the Heisman Trophy? Archie Griffin

103. In what year did the first Indianapolis 500 take place? 1911

104. Who was the first player to win an NBA Championship in three different decades? John Salley

105. Who is the only person to win a Super Bowl and Rose Bowl as a head coach? Dick Vermeil

106. In 1896, Harold Mahoney was the first Scottish player to win what tournament? Wimbledon

107. What NFL Hall of Famer was an outfielder for the 1919 New York Yankees? George Halas

108. What former MLB pitcher holds the record for surrendering the most all-time home runs? Jamie Moyer

109. What is the diameter of a regulation basketball hoop? 18 inches

110. What is the national sport of Ireland? Hurling

111. What professional soccer club did Gordon Ramsey play for before becoming a chef? Glasgow Rangers

112. Who holds the record for the most wins as an NFL head coach? Don Shula

113. How many feet long is a regulation NBA basketball court? 94 feet

114. Who has won the most Formula One World Drivers' Championships? Michael Schumacher (7)

115. In what season did the NBA begin using the 3-point line? 1979-1980

116. Who holds the MLB record for the most career strike outs as a batter? Reggie Jackson

117. What sport is played in seven-minute periods called Chukkas? Polo

118. Who was the first NBA player to score 30,000 points? Wilt Chamberlin

119. Who holds the record for the most passing yards in an NFL game? Norm Van Brocklin

120. Where did Julius Erving play collegiate basketball? University of Massachusetts

121. Who was World Heavyweight Boxing Champion from 1919 to 1926? Jack Dempsey

122. Which Austrian city hosted the Winter Olympic Games in 1964 and 1976? Innsbruck

123. Which NBA team drafted Kobe Bryant? Charlotte Hornets

124. Which USFL team did Herschel Walker play for? New Jersey Generals

125. How many events make up a decathlon? 10

126. How many minutes are in a European football (soccer) match? 90

127. How many players are on the field at one time in a men's lacrosse game? 20

128. Lionel Messi plays for which country in international soccer competitions? Argentina

129. Which MLB team holds the record for the most wins in a single season? Seattle Mariners

130. What professional soccer club plays its home games at Old Trafford? Manchester United

131. Who is the youngest NFL quarterback to throw for 5,000 yards in a season? Matthew Stafford

132. Who is the only player in NBA history to record a double-triple-double? Wilt Chamberlin

133. In what year, did boxing become a legal sport in the U.S.? 1901

134. Who was head coach of the 1980 Olympic hockey team? Herb Brooks

135. What sport uses the Stableford scoring system? Golf

136. Who was the first figure skater to land a quadruple jump in competition? Kurt Browning

137. Who was the first African American to hit a home run in the World Series? Larry Doby

138. Who was the first Canadian born player to be drafted #1 overall in the NBA draft? Anthony Bennett

139. Who was the first head coach to win both an NCAA Championship and an NBA Championship? Larry Brown

140. What football player was known as "The Galloping Ghost"? Red Grange

141. A velodrome hosts what kind of sporting event? Cycling

142. In what year was the first college football game played? 1869

143. What is golfer Tiger Woods' first name? Eldrick

144. Who was the first NHL player to score 50 goals in 50 games? Maurice Richard

145. Which MLB team won the most division titles in the 1990's? Atlanta Braves

146. What speed skater won five individual gold medals at the 1980 Winter Olympics? Eric Heiden

147. What is the name of the long log tossed in Highland Games? Caber

148. In what year was the first Boston Marathon ran? 1897

149. The Maurice Podoloff Trophy is awarded annually to the MVP in which professional sports league? National Basketball Association (NBA)

150. In standard billiards, what color is the #2 ball? Blue

A Literary Mind

1. In what year was the first issue of *National Geographic* magazine published? 1888
2. What novel by Ken Follett tells the 12th century story of the building of a cathedral in Kingsbridge, England? The Pillars of the Earth
3. In what year was *Alice's Adventures in Wonderland* published? 1865
4. How many books make up the *Chronicles of Narnia* by C.S. Lewis? Seven
5. Nick Carraway is the narrator in what novel? The Great Gatsby
6. Who wrote *Across the River* and *Into the Trees*? Ernest Hemingway
7. Who wrote *The Old Curiosity Shop*? Charles Dickens
8. How many nights are in the novel, *Arabian Nights*? 1,001
9. How many syllables comprise a Haiku? 17
10. Who wrote *The Martian Chronicles*? Ray Bradbury
11. Ernest Hemingway's *For Whom the Bell Tolls* is based on his experiences during which war? Spanish Civil War
12. Who wrote the 1855 poem *The Song of Hiawatha*? Henry Wadsworth Longfellow

13. What was the first cartoon strip to win a Pulitzer Prize? Doonesbury

14. What book was based off the real life of Alexander Selkirk? Robinson Crusoe

15. Who was the first American to win the Nobel Prize in Literature? Sinclair Lewis

16. What novel features Lennie Small? Of Mice and Men

17. What is J.R.R. Tolkien's full name? John Ronald Reuel Tolkien

18. Who wrote *The Bourne Identity*? Robert Ludlum

19. What title is held by the character Edmund Dantes in a novel by Alexander Dumas? The Count of Monte Cristo

20. Edward Nigma is the real name of which comic book villain? Riddler

21. In *The Da Vinci Code*, at what school is Robert Langdon a professor? Harvard

22. Who was the first African American woman to win a Pulitzer Prize? Gwendolyn Brooks

23. Who writes the *Game of Thrones* series? George R. R. Martin

24. Who received the 1929 Nobel Prize in Literature for his novel, *Buddenbrooks*? Thomas Mann

25. Who wrote *50 Shades of Grey*? E.L. James

26. In what language, did Anne Frank write her famed diary? Dutch

27. Who wrote the 1963 novel, *Ice Station Zebra*? Alistair MacLean

28. What book did Mark David Chapman read while waiting to be arrested after he murdered John Lennon? The Catcher in the Rye

29. Who wrote *Fight Club*? Chuck Palahniuk

30. Who found the fourth Golden Ticket in *Charlie and the Chocolate Factory*? Mike Teavee

31. Who wrote *The Hitchhiker's Guide to the Galaxy*? Douglas Adams

32. *Captain! My Captain!* is a poem written by whom? Walt Whitman

33. In *The Lion, The Witch and The Wardrobe*, what type of creature is Maugrim? Wolf

34. What poem tells of a sailor cursed for shooting an albatross? The Rime of the Ancient Mariner

35. Who wrote *The Picture of Dorian Grey*? Oscar Wilde

36. In *Madame Bovary*, what is Mrs. Bovary's first name? Emma

37. Who wrote the 2008 novel, *The Hunger Games*? Suzanne Collins

38. What book by E.M. Forster surrounds the Wilcox, Schlegel and Bast families? Howards End

39. Who wrote *Catch-22*? Joseph Heller

40. In the comic "Peanuts", what is the last name of Lucy and Linus? Van Pelt

41. In Rudyard Kipling's *The Jungle Book*, what is the name of the black panther? Bagheera

42. Tess Trueheart is the wife of what comic strip character? Dick Tracy

43. Atticus Finch is the main character in which novel by Harper Lee? To Kill a Mockingbird

44. Who wrote *Battlefield Earth*? L. Ron Hubbard

45. What is the professor's name in *Lolita* who becomes involved with Dolores Haze? Humbert Humber

46. Who wrote *A Streetcar Named Desire*? Tennessee Williams

47. *Eagle Strike, Snakehead and Point Blanc* are all novels in a series about what youth spy? Alex Rider

48. Who wrote *The Da Vinci Code*? Dan Brown

49. What was the name of the hitman in *No Country for Old Men*? Anton Chigurh

50. Who was voted "The Chief" in *Lord of the Flies*? Ralph

51. For which U.S. newspaper was Karl Marx once a correspondent? *New York Tribune*

52. What was the first book picked for Oprah's Book Club? The Deep End of the Ocean

53. What does Hogwart's motto, "Draco dormiens nunquam titillandus" mean? "Never tickle a sleeping dragon."

54. Who wrote *Atlas Shrugged*? Ayn Rand

55. In *Animal Farm* by George Orwell, what type of animal is Napoleon? Pig

56. Who wrote the 1996 novel, *Infinite Jest*? David Foster Wallace

57. Who was on the first cover of *People* magazine? Mia Farrow

58. What is the name of William Shakespeare's longest play? Hamlet

59. What 1961 novel by Robert A. Heinlein tells the story of a Martian named Valentine Michael Smith? *Stranger in a Strange Land*

60. What novella was first published as *Der Tod in Venedig*? Death in Venice

61. What country is the setting for the dinosaur park in *Jurassic Park*? Costa Rica

62. What is Scarlett O'Hara's real first name in *Gone with the Wind*? Katie

63. Who is the author of the *Sherlock Holmes* series of books? Sir Arthur Conan Doyle

64. Whose last words before he drank poison reportedly were, "Crito, we owe a cock to Asclepius. Pay it and do not neglect it?" Socrates

65. Gabilan is the title animal of which John Steinbeck novel? The Red Pony

66. What American poet was court martialed in 1830? Edgar Allen Poe

67. Who is the King of Rohan in *The Lord of the Rings*? Theoden

68. What bear did A.A. Milne create? Winnie the Pooh

69. Who wrote the *Ramona Quimby* series? Beverly Cleary

70. Cobweb is a fairy in which Shakespeare play? A Midsummer Night's Dream

71. What physicist wrote, *A Brief History of Time*? Stephen Hawkins

72. What language was *The Girl with the Dragon Tattoo* first written in? Swedish

73. In what year was the first edition of *Playboy* magazine published? 1953

74. What author wrote romance novels using the pen name, Mary Westmacott? Agatha Christie

75. In *Charlotte's Webb*, what is Charlotte's last name? Cavatica

76. What poem by John Milton tells the Biblical story of Adam and Eve's temptation and the Fall of Man? Paradise Lost

77. What was the name of Rip Van Winkle's dog? Wolf

78. Who wrote *Treasure Island*? Robert Louis Stevenson

79. How many years did it take Leo Tolstoy to write *War & Peace*? 6

80. What institution awards Pulitzer Prizes? Columbia University

81. Who wrote *Pygmalion*? George Bernard Shaw

82. During what war is *The Lion, the Witch and the Wardrobe* set to? World War II

83. Who wrote the pamphlet "Common Sense" in 1776? Thomas Paine

84. How old is Juliet in *Romeo and Juliet*? 13

85. In how many categories is the Pulitzer Prize awarded? 21

86. Who wrote the children's book, *The Trumpeter Swan*? E.B. White

87. What was the first play written by an African American woman to be produced on Broadway? A Raisin in the Sun

88. What book series tells the story of the five factions: Abnegation, Amity, Candor, Dauntless, and Erudite? Divergent

89. What poet wrote *A Child's Christmas in Wales*? Dylan Thomas

90. In poetry, how many lines traditionally make up a villanelle? 19

91. Who wrote *Frankenstein* in 1818? Mary Shelley

92. What was Ichabod Crane's profession in *The Legend of Sleepy Hollow*? Teacher

93. Who wrote *Mary Poppins*? P.L. Travers

94. "When he woke in woods in the dark and the cold of the night he'd reach out to touch the child sleeping beside him," is the opening line to what novel? The Road

95. In which James Joyce novel is Leopold Bloom the main character? w

96. Who wrote "Letter from Birmingham Jail?" Martin Luther King Jr.

97. What is the name of the runt rabbit in *Watership Down*? Fiver

98. How many books comprise the "New Testament"? 27

99. What was the first novel ever written on a typewriter? Tom Sawyer

100. Who wrote *Doctor Zhivago*? Boris Pasternak

101. What was the first book to win the Nebula Award for Best Novel? Dune

102. Who is the main female character in *Eat, Pray, Love*? Elizabeth Gilbert

103. Who was the first actor to appear on the cover of *Time* magazine? Charlie Chaplin

104. In what year was *The Great Gatsby* published? 1925

105. When is Harry Potter's birthday? July 31

106. In what Jane Austen novel is Mr. Darcy a main character? Pride and Prejudice

107. What novel by S.E. Hinton was later made into a movie starring Patrick Swayze and C. Thomas Howell? The Outsiders

108. Who wrote *Wuthering Heights*? Emily Bronte

109. Who did Dante choose to guide him through hell and purgatory in *The Divine Comedy*? Virgil

110. What was Sylvia Plath's only novel? The Bell Jar

111. What novel by Fyodor Dostoyevsky tells the story of ex-student Rodion Raskolnikov? Crime and Punishment

112. What was Barbara Taylor Bradford's debut novel? A Woman of Substance

113. How old was Scarlett O'Hara at the start of *Gone with the Wind*? 16

114. What novel featured, The Whiskey Priest? The Power and the Glory

115. Who wrote *Breakfast at Tiffany's*? Truman Capote

116. In *Twilight*, what is Jacob's last name? Black

117. "As Gregor Samsa awoke one morning from uneasy dreams he found himself transformed in his bed into a gigantic insect," is the open line to what novel? The Metamorphosis

118. What was the first Alexandre Dumas novel to feature the characters, Athos, Aramis and Porthos? The Three Musketeers

119. What is the name of the novel about a prince who travels on an asteroid? The Little Prince

120. Tommy and Annika are the best friends of which literary character? Pippi Longstocking

121. What novel tells the story of firefighters burning down any house containing books? Fahrenheit 451

122. Sophie Zawistowska is the title character in which William Styron novel? Sophie's Choice

123. Who wrote *Brave New World* and *The Doors*? Aldous Huxley

124. Bucky or Winter Soldier is which literary character's sidekick? Captain America

125. What was Charles Lutwidge Dodgson's pen name? Lewis Carroll

The "G" in Geography

1. What is the world's largest landlocked country? Kazakhstan

2. How many U.S. states border the Pacific Ocean? 5

3. Which U.S. state is closest to Bermuda? North Carolina

4. In which U.S. state is Glacier National Park located? Montana

5. What is Canada's oldest city? Quebec

6. In what country is the Ring of Brodgar located? Scotland

7. What is the name of the sea that lies between Israel and Jordan? Dead Sea

8. How many U.S. states share a land or water border with Canada? 13

9. What is the only European capital city not located on a river? Madrid

10. What country is completely landlocked within the Republic of South Africa? Lesotho

11. Lake Ontario is the source for which river? St. Lawrence River

12. What is the largest lake located entirely within a single, U.S. state? Great Salt Lake

13. Which city had the world's first paved streets? Rome, Italy

14. In which European country is Balmoral Castle located? Scotland

15. What is the capital of the Czech Republic? Prague

16. What is the name of the island which lies in the middle of the Niagara Falls? Goat Island

17. What is the only country that borders both Venezuela and Paraguay? Peru

18. What country is almost completely surrounded by Senegal? Gambia

19. What country has Europe's highest capital city? Andorra

20. Ouagadougou is the capital of what country? Burkina Faso

21. What is the world's smallest ocean? Arctic Ocean

22. Which Canadian territory sits closest to the North Pole? Nunavut

23. In which European city is Brandenburg Gate located? Berlin

24. What mountain is nicknamed Savage Mountain? K2

25. What is the longest river in Europe? Volga

26. What country has the most time zones? Russia

27. Which U.S. city is known as the City of Roses?
Portland, OR

28. What is the world's only sea without a coastline?
Sargasso Sea

29. What is the only country with three official capitals?
South Africa

30. In which city is the Wailing Wall (Western Wall)
located? Jerusalem

31. What is the world's largest archipelago? Indonesia

32. How many U.S. states have four-letter names? 3

33. Which country has the most pyramids? Peru

34. Which U.S. state has the least number of counties?
Delaware (3)

35. What volcanic eruption destroyed the Roman cities of
Pompeii and Herculaneum? Mount Vesuvius

36. What is the only U.S. state that has a one syllable
name? Maine

37. Which island was previously named Van Diemen's
Land? Tasmania

38. What is the capital of Belarus? Minsk

39. In which U.S. state is Cochiti Dam located? New
Mexico

40. What is the capital of Ivory Coast? Yamoussoukro

41. How many U.S. state capitals are named after U.S. Presidents? 4

42. In which U.S. state is Lake Francis Case located? South Dakota

43. Burma is the former name of which Asian country? Myanmar

44. What is the only state that borders just one other state? Maine

45. What is the capital of North Korea? Pyongyang

46. What is the world's most densely populated country? Monaco

47. In which country is Petra located? Jordan

48. In which European city is the Bridge of Sighs located? Venice, Italy

49. Lake Titicaca lies on the border of Bolivia and what other country? Peru

50. In what European city is the Arch of Hadrian? Athens

51. What country is the world's largest producer of vanilla beans? Madagascar

52. Which U.S. state is the largest producer of eggplants? New Jersey

53. Which non-landlocked country has the shortest coastline? Monaco

54. What city is home to NATO headquarters? Brussels, Belgium

55. What is the capital of Canada? Ottawa

56. In which U.S. state is Bryce Canyon National Park located? Utah

57. How many U.S. states border the Gulf of Mexico? 5

58. What country is the world's largest cotton producer? China

59. In what country is Chalbi Desert located? Kenya

60. In which U.S. state is the Klickitat River? Washington

61. What is the largest lake located entirely within Canada? Great Bear Lake

62. Mount Kosciuszko is the highest mountain on which continent? Australia

63. How many U.S. states have X in their name? 2

64. Which Russian city was called Stalingrad from 1925-1961? Volgograd

65. How many floors does the Empire State Building have? 102

66. What country was formerly known as British Honduras? Belize

67. What city is the headquarters for Interpol? Lyon, France

68. Which U.S. state is nicknamed the Beehive State? Utah

69. What South American city is nicknamed the City of Drizzle? Sao Paulo, Brazil

70. What place in the U.S. sits 282 feet below sea level? Death Valley

71. What is the capital of West Virginia? Charleston

72. What continent gets the least amount of precipitation each year? Antarctica

73. What is the world's highest plateau? Tibetan Plateau

74. What is the capital of Qatar? Doha

75. In terms of total area, what is the largest country in Africa? Algeria

76. Which is the only U.S. state that does not have land designated for a national park? Delaware

77. What is the only continent without an active volcano? Australia

78. What is the only U.S. state not to have a straight line in its border? Hawaii

79. What is the largest country with only one time zone? China

80. In what country is Sugarloaf Mountain located? Brazil

81. What is the world's oldest inhabited city? Damascus, Syria

82. What is the only state that produces coffee? Hawaii

83. In what country is Great Victoria Desert located? Australia

84. What are the only mobile U.S. National Monuments? San Francisco Cable Cars

85. What is the largest island that is crossed by the Arctic Circle? Greenland

86. What city has the largest port in Europe? Rotterdam

87. What was the original name of Hoover Dam? Boulder Dam

88. Regina is the capital of which Canadian province? Saskatchewan

89. What is Mexico's largest state? Chihuahua

90. What is the largest country that the equator passes through? Brazil

91. What is the capital of Nicaragua? Managua

92. What is the official currency of China? Yuan

93. What is the world's largest man-made structure? Great Wall of China

94. What country was previously called Abyssinia? Ethiopia

95. What is Europe's largest island? Great Britain

96. What is the longest interstate highway in the U.S.? I-90

97. What is the only country that falls in all four hemispheres? Kiribati

98. In what U.S. state is Cat River located? Minnesota

99. In what desert is Grand Erg Oriental located? Sahara Desert

100. Which U.S. state is nicknamed the Crossroads of America? Indiana

101. In which country is Serengeti National Park located? Tanzania

102. What is the world's largest park? Northeast Greenland National Park

103. Borah Peak is the highest mountain in which U.S. state? Idaho

104. What Central American country's name means 'many fish'? Panama

105. What is the only U.S. state named after an English county? New Hampshire

106. In what country is Atacama Desert located? Chile

107. Harlem, NY is named after a city in which country? Netherlands

108. What is the only U.S. state that shares its name with an independent country? Georgia

109. What is the only Central American country with English as its official language? Belize

110. What is the capital of Liechtenstein? Vaduz

111. What is the most populous country in the world situated only on islands? Indonesia

112. The Grand Coulee Dam uses the power of which river to produce hydroelectricity? Columbia River

113. What mountain has three volcanic cones; Kibo, Shira and Mawenzi? Mt. Kilimanjaro

114. The Galapagos Islands are part of which country? Ecuador

115. What is the name for the group of islands that lie off the coast of Normandy, France? Channel Islands

116. What country is known as the "Land of White Elephant"? Thailand

117. Easter Island is a territory belonging to what country? Chile

118. Which is the only U.S. state whose eastern and western borders are rivers? Iowa

119. Montevideo is the capital of which country? Uruguay

120. What is the world's tallest pyramid? The Great Pyramid of Giza

121. In what county is the temple Angkor Wat located? Cambodia

122. What is the largest country located entirely in Europe? Ukraine

123. How many countries sit on the equator? 13

124. How many different time zones are there in the world? 24

125. In what country is Timbuktu located? Mali

126. In which U.S. state is Joshua Tree National Park located? California

127. Which U.S. state has the longest land border with Canada? Alaska

128. What is the largest island of The Bahamas? Andros

129. In which country is Volcano Park located? Germany

130. On what island is the volcano Hekla located? Iceland

131. What island is also known as Rapa Nui? Easter Island

132. What is the world's lowest country? The Maldives

133. In which city is John Lennon Wall located? Prague

134. In which city is the International Criminal Court located? The Hague

135. The pyramids the Sun and the Moon are located, in which country? Mexico

136. What country borders Estonia from the south? Latvia

137. In which body of water is the Great Barrier Reef located? Coral Sea

138. What is the world's largest, landlocked harbor? San Francisco Bay

139. What is the capital of Montana? Helena

140. Which U.S. state has the smallest population? Wyoming

141. Which U.S. state is home to The Pentagon? Virginia

142. Which capital city touches two continents? Istanbul

143. What is the capital of Macedonia? Skopje

144. What is the only U.S. state to not share any letters with its capital city's name? South Dakota

145. What country is the world's largest producer of coffee beans? Brazil

146. If you were facing Mount Rushmore, which U.S. President would be furthest to your right? Abraham Lincoln

147. In which ocean is Chukchi Sea located? Arctic Ocean

148. What is the world's deepest lake? Lake Baikal

149. What is the official language of Liechtenstein? German

150. In what city is Cleopatra's Needle located? London, England

151. What is the name of the church located in Moscow's Red Square? St. Basil's Cathedral

152. What was the original name of New York City? New Amsterdam

153. What country has the world's largest coastline? Canada

154. How many states border the Mississippi river? 10

155. Between 1949 and 1990, what city was the capital of West Germany? Bonn

156. What was the first U.S. National Monument? Devils Tower

157. The Strawberry Fields memorial is located inside which U.S. Park? New York City's Central Park

158. How many states does the Appalachian Train run through? 14

159. What is the English name for the resort area of Côte d'Azur? French Riviera

160. What country's two main islands are separated by Cook Strait? New Zealand

161. How tall is Mount Everest? 29,029 feet

162. What is the world's largest mountain chain? Mid-Atlantic Ridge

163. What city is The Forbidden City of Tibet? Lhasa

164. How many Great Lakes are there? 5

165. In which country is Euromast is located? Netherlands

166. What peninsula do Spain and Portugal form? Iberian Peninsula

167. Freetown is the capital of which African country? Sierra Leone

168. A snake and what other, animal is displayed on Mexico's flag? Eagle

169. Which U.S. National Park is home to Bridal Veil Falls? Yosemite National Park

170. In which European city is Monument of Light located? Dublin, Ireland

171. What connects the Red Sea to the Mediterranean Sea? Suez Canal

172. How many degrees of east longitude are there? 180 degrees

173. What country's name was originally Ceylon? Sri Lanka

174. How many provinces does Canada have? 10

175. Ellsworth Mountains are located on which continent? Antarctica

176. Zagreb is the capital of which country? Croatia

177. What is the largest island in the Mediterranean Sea? Sicily

178. What is the largest landmass that lies entirely in the Pacific Ocean? New Guinea

179. How many countries start with Q? 1 (Qatar)

180. How many U.S. states do not border either a Great Lake or ocean? 20

181. Into which sea does the Nile River empty? Mediterranean Sea

182. What city is home to the world's longest street? Toronto

183. What is the southernmost city in the continental United States? Key West, FL

184. What is the largest body of fresh water in the world? Lake Superior

185. Which U.S. state has the most counties? Texas

186. What is the world's smallest island country? Nauru

187. What is the capital of Ecuador? Quito

188. What city is home to the Unisphere? New York City

189. What is the world's largest desert? Antarctica

190. What is the tallest volcano in the continental United States? Mount Rainier

191. How many miles long is the Grand Canyon? 277 miles

192. Bombay is the former name of what city in India? Mumbai

193. In what country is the world's largest fjord located? Greenland

194. What is the only country on the South American continent that starts with the letter S? Suriname

195. In what city is the Space Needle located? Seattle, WA

196. How many U.S. states have capitals that begin with the same letter? 4

197. What country has more lakes than all the world's other countries combined? Canada

198. What world city is home to Kew Gardens? London, England

199. In what city is Copacabana beach located? Rio de Janeiro

200. Which U.S. state is home to Thermopolis Hot Springs? Wyoming

U.S. Presidents for the Win

1. Which President was once an ambassador to the United Nations and Director of the CIA? George H. W. Bush

2. Who was the only man to become both Vice President and President after resignations? Gerald Ford

3. Who was the first President to serve two, non-consecutive terms? Grover Cleveland

4. Who is the only President to have a U.S. National Park named after him? William McKinley

5. Who was the last President to have facial hair? William Howard Taft

6. Which President was assassinated by Charles Julius Guiteau? James Garfield

7. Who was the first President to lose both the popular and electoral votes in the same election? John Quincy Adams

8. How many Presidents have been named James? 6

9. Who was the last President born in the 19th century? Dwight D. Eisenhower

10. What was George Washington's annual salary as President? $25,000

11. Who is the only President to never sign a bill into law? William Henry Harrison

12. Who was the first President born in a hospital? Jimmy Carter

13. Which U.S. state has been the birthplace to the most Presidents? Virginia

14. What was President Ronald Reagan's Secret Service codename? Rawhide

15. Who was the first President to have been a Rhodes Scholar? Bill Clinton

16. Who was the last bachelor President? James Buchanan

17. Which President later became Chief Justice of the United States Supreme Court? William Howard Taft

18. What is the minimum age to be elected U.S. President? 35

19. How many Presidents have served as a U.S. state governor? 17

20. What type of gun did John Wilkes Booth use to assassinate Abraham Lincoln? Philadelphia Derringer

21. Who was the first President to win a Nobel Prize? Teddy Roosevelt

22. Who was the first President to win a Pulitzer Prize? John F. Kennedy

23. Who has been the shortest President? James Madison

24. Which President's high school nickname was Barry O'Bomber? Barack Obama

25. Who was the first President to visit all 50 U.S. states? Richard Nixon

26. Who was the first President to live in the White House? John Adams

27. Who is the only President to have been born on the 4th of July? Calvin Coolidge

28. Which President was on the $5,000 bill? James Madison

29. Who was the first Vice-President to become President after the death of a President in office? John Tyler

30. Which President was once a teacher? Lyndon Johnson

31. What college did Thomas Jefferson found? University of Virginia

32. Who was the first president to earn a PhD? Woodrow Wilson

33. Which President had the most children? John Tyler

34. Which President was the first to be born a U.S. citizen? Martin Van Buren

35. What is Rutherford B. Hayes middle name? Birchard

36. Big Bill was the nickname of which President? William Taft

37. Who was the first President to have electricity installed in the White House? Benjamin Harrison

38. Which President was arrested for running over a woman with his carriage? Franklin Pierce

39. Which President remarried Rachel Donelson Robards? Andrew Jackson

40. Who was the first President to talk on a phone? James Garfield

41. Which President was once a high school cheerleader? George W. Bush

42. How many Presidents had previously been U.S. Vice President? 14

43. Which President was once a tailor? Andrew Johnson

44. Who was the first President to make a radio broadcast? Calvin Coolidge

45. Which President died from contracting cholera? Zachary Taylor

46. Who was the first President to have his picture taken during his presidency? James Polk

47. Which President was shot while giving a speech in Milwaukee, WI? Teddy Roosevelt

48. Which President married his former teacher? Millard Fillmore

49. Who was the first President to appear on television? Franklin D. Roosevelt

50. Who was the first President to see the Pacific Ocean in person? Ulysses S. Grant

Talk about the Body

1. What is the longest bone in the body? Femur

2. How many pairs of cranial nerves are in the body? 12

3. What is Mydriasis? Pupil widening

4. What is the most common blood type? O Positive

5. What is the fastest healing muscle in the body? Tongue

6. What is the largest internal organ? Small intestine

7. Rickets is primarily caused due to a deficiency in which vitamin? Vitamin D

8. Which part of the body is most sensitive to radiation? Blood

9. What fatal disease is associated with aspirin consumption by children? Reye's Syndrome

10. What is the medical term for high blood pressure? Hypertension

11. What is the longest vein in the body? Great Saphenous vein

12. The medical condition Herpes Zoster is commonly known as what? Shingles

13. What is the medical name for the big toe? Hallux

14. What is the name for the liquid part of blood? Plasma

15. In the brain, what is the area that is involved in language processing, speech production and comprehension? Broca's Area

16. What is Bovine Spongiform Encephalopathy more commonly known as? Mad Cow Disease

17. What is the smallest bone in the body? Stapes

18. What is the medical term for an inflamed throat? Pharyngitis

19. What is the medical term for not being able to smell? Anosmia

20. If someone has Pyrosis, what medical condition do they have? Heartburn

21. In what year did the world's first sex-change operation take place? 1952

22. Alopecia is the medical term for what? Hair loss

23. What is the depressed area of skin under your nose and above your upper lip called? Philtrum

24. What type of cell is a leukocyte? White Blood Cell

25. What is the name for the group of fibers that connects the brain's left and right hemispheres? Corpus Callosum

26. Quinsy is a medical complication affecting which body part? Tonsils

27. What is the longest muscle in the body? Sartorius

28. What is the small, pink spot in the corner of the eye called? Caruncula

29. Cholera is an infection affecting which organ? Small intestine

30. What is the outer layer of the skin called? Epidermis

31. Metritis is the inflammation of which body part? Uterus

32. What does a Noctambulist do? Sleepwalk

33. What bone connects the humerus with the clavicle? Scapula

34. How many different blood groups do humans have? 4

35. What is Hansen's disease more commonly called? Leprosy

36. Myocardium is the muscular tissue surrounding which organ? Heart

37. How many pairs of chromosomes does a human usually have? 23

38. On what part of the eye does a Cataract develop? Lens

39. What organ produces insulin? Pancreas

40. Where is the Fissure of Roland located? Brain

41. What does someone have if they have the Varicella Zoster virus? Chickenpox

42. A deficiency in what element can lead to Goiter? Iodine

43. What organ uses Purkinje fibers? Heart

44. The cartilage in the knee is generally referred to as what? Meniscus

45. Ageusia is the loss of which of the five senses? Taste

46. Nephrosis is the degeneration of which organ? Kidneys

47. What bodily fluid is collected in a lachrymatory? Tears

48. How many joints does an adult human have? 360

49. What are the ridges in the cerebrum called? Gyri

50. In what organ is the Bundle of His located? Heart

51. What is the fastest growing organ? Liver

52. What does a Sphygmomanometer measure? Blood pressure

53. What is someone doing if they are Micturating? Urinating

54. What is the most abundant mineral in the body? Calcium

55. What is the medical term for the knee cap? Patella

56. How many bones are in the hand? 27

57. What is the longest nerve in the body? Sciatic nerve

58. What is the only part of the body without a blood supply? Cornea

59. Where in a cell does protein synthesis occur? Ribosome

60. How many pairs of ribs does an adult have? 12

61. What is the fastest healing tissues in the body? Cornea

62. In what organ is the Loop of Henle located? Kidney

63. What is the largest blood vessel in the body? Aorta

64. What type of body part connects muscle to bone? Tendon

65. What is the most abundant naturally occurring amino acid in the body? Glutamine

66. What is the only jointless bone in the body? Hyoid bone

67. In what part of the body is Alcock's canal? Pelvis

68. What is the space between someone's eyebrows called? Glabella

69. What is the body's shortest muscle? Stapedius

70. What is the name of the pigment that gives skin its color? Melanin

71. Where are red blood cells produced? Bone marrow

72. What is the attachment of muscles to skin called? Dimples

73. What are the body's fast growing hairs? Facial hairs

74. What part of the brain controls food intake? Hypothalamus

75. How many valves are in the heart? 4

76. What is the most abundant enzyme in saliva? Amylase

77. What do Goblet cells secrete? Mucin

78. What do seminiferous tubules produce? Sperm

79. What is the ability to sense position and location called? Proprioception

80. What organ produces bile? Liver

81. What does someone have if they have Pes Planus? Flatfoot

82. What is the only muscle attached at one end? Tongue

83. What is the body's strongest substance? Tooth enamel

84. What organ secretes cortisol? Adrenal gland

85. In which organ are the Islets of Langerhans located? Pancreas

86. How many layers does skin have? 2

87. What organ system does the spleen belong to? Lymphatic system

88. What is the medical condition Synchronous Diaphragmatic Flutter more commonly known as? Hiccups

89. Where is the ethmoid bone located? Skull

90. Compression of which nerve causes Carpel Tunnel Syndrome? Median nerve

91. In what part of the eye are cones and rods located? Retina

92. What is the Pollex? Thumb

93. Which gland produces Melatonin? Pineal gland

94. What is the most abundant substance in the brain? Water

95. What is the white part of a fingernail called? Lunula

96. What is the Umbilicus more commonly referred to as? Navel

97. How many fused vertebrate does a human typically have? 9

98. What is the medical term for the hip bone? Coxal bone

99. What is the name of the fluid that lubricates and cushions joints between bones? Synovial fluid

100. In what organ are Alveoli located? Lung

Who Said It?

1. "I will fight no more, forever." Chief Joseph of the Nez Perce

2. "I don't see why we need to stand by and watch a country go Communist because of the irresponsibility of its own people." Henry Kissinger

3. "We have met the enemy and they are ours." Oliver Hazard Perry

4. "I'm not worried about anything; I'm not fearing any man." Martin Luther King Jr.

5. "Let your food be your medicine, and your medicine be your food." Hippocrates

6. "How wonderful it is that nobody need wait a single moment before starting to improve the world." Anne Frank

7. "You can't connect the dots looking forward; you can only connect them looking backwards. So you have to trust that the dots will somehow connect in your future. You have to trust in something – your gut, destiny, life, karma, whatever. This approach has never let me down, and it has made all the difference in my life." Steve Jobs

8. "It is our choices that show what we truly are, far more than our abilities." J.K. Rowling

9. "It is not in the stars to hold our destiny but in ourselves." William Shakespeare

10. "Loneliness and the feeling of being unwanted is the most terrible poverty." Mother Teresa

11. "I took a speed reading course and read *War and Peace* in twenty minutes. It involves Russia." Woody Allen

12. "Every great dream begins with a dreamer. Always remember, you have within you the strength, the patience, and the passion to reach for the stars to change the world." Harriet Tubman

13. "So many books, so little time." Frank Zappa

14. "Be who you are and say what you feel, because those who mind don't matter, and those who matter don't mind." Bernard M. Baruch

15. "Being a princess isn't all it's cracked up to be." Princess Diana

16. "The opposite of talking isn't listening. The opposite of talking is waiting." Fran Lebowitz

17. "It is better to light a candle than curse the darkness." Eleanor Roosevelt

18. "Those who believe in telekinetics, raise my hand." Kurt Vonnegut

19. "You only live once, but if you do it right, once is enough." Mae West

20. "Christmas is a season for kindling the fire for hospitality in the hall, the genial flame of charity in the heart." Washington Irving

21. "Military intelligence is a contradiction in terms." Groucho Marx

22. "To be yourself in a world that is constantly trying to make you something else is the greatest accomplishment." Ralph Waldo Emerson

23. "The real voyage of discovery consists not in seeking new lands but seeing with new eyes." Marcel Proust

24. "When I was a boy I was told that anybody could become President. Now I'm beginning to believe it." Clarence Darrow

25. "Some people feel the rain. Others just get wet." Bob Marley

26. "It is the mark of an educated mind to be able to entertain a thought without accepting it." Aristotle

27. "Truth is so rare that it is delightful to tell it." Emily Dickinson

28. "The greatest minds are capable of the greatest vices as well as of the greatest virtues." Rene Descartes

29. "There are people who have money and people who are rich." Coco Chanel

30. "I believe a leaf of grass is no less than the journey-work of the stars." Walt Whitman

31. "What loneliness is more lonely than distrust?" George Eliot

32. "The government solution to a problem is usually as bad as the problem." Milton Friedman

33. "I still have my feet on the ground, I just wear better shoes." Oprah Winfrey

34. "It is kind of fun to do the impossible." Walt Disney

35. "The older one grows, the more one like's indecency." Virginia Woolf

36. "Insanity: doing the same thing over and over again and expecting different results." Albert Einstein

37. "Let him that would move the world first move himself." Socrates

38. "There are two means of refuge from the miseries of life: music and cats." Albert Schweitzer

39. "Be careful when you fight the monsters, lest you become one." Friedrich Nietzsche

40. "Do not hire a man who does your work for money, but him who does it for love of it." Henry David Thoreau

41. "Always forgive your enemies; nothing annoys them so much." Oscar Wilde

42. "An ounce of practice is worth more than tons of preaching." Mahatma Gandhi

43. "If you're going to be two-faced at least make one of them pretty." Marilyn Monroe

44. "Whatever you are. Be a good one." Abraham Lincoln

45. "Everything has its beauty, but not everyone sees it." Confucius

46. "Don't cry because it's over, smile because it happened." Dr. Seuss

47. "Walking with a friend in the dark is better than walking alone in the light." Helen Keller

48. "Sleep is the best meditation." Dalai Lama

49. "Go to Heaven for the climate, Hell for the company." Mark Twain

50. "The tongue like a sharp knife... Kills without drawing blood." Buddha

Acronyms from A to Z

1. NASA – National Aeronautical Space Administration
2. EKG (Medicine) – Electrocardiogram
3. LZ (Military) – Landing Zone
4. UNICEF - United Nations Children's Fund
5. HTML - HyperText Markup Language
6. LASER (Science) - Light Amplification by Stimulated Emission of Radiation
7. NATO - North Atlantic Treaty Organization
8. RADAR – Radio Detection and Ranging
9. HIPAA - Health Insurance Portability and Accountability Act
10. RNA (Biology) - Ribonucleic acid
11. SCUBA – Self-Contained Underwater Breathing Apparatus
12. JPEG - Joint Photographic Experts Group
13. CBGB (Music Venue) - Country, Bluegrass, and Blues
14. WFTU - World Federation of Trade Unions
15. OPEC - Organization of the Petroleum Exporting Countries
16. POTUS - President of the United States
17. RAM (Computer) - Random Access Memory

18. CNBC (Cable Television) - Consumer News and Business Channel
19. TEOTWAWKI - The End Of The World As We Know It
20. IQ - Intelligence Quotient
21. Special Weapons and Tactics – Special Weapons and Tactics
22. HIV - Human Immunodeficiency Virus
23. LED - Light Emitting Diode
24. AM (Radio) - Amplitude Modification
25. CAT (Scan) - Computer Assisted Tomography
26. ISBN - International Standard Book Number
27. GMO (Food) - Genetically Modified
28. SONAR – Sound Navigation and Ranging
29. CPR - Cardiopulmonary Resuscitation
30. NAFTA - North American Free Trade Agreement
31. PSI (Physics) - Pounds Per Square Inch
32. A.D. (Time) - Anno Domini
33. HTTP - Hypertext Transfer Protocol
34. EEG (Medicine) – Electroencephalography
35. NAACP - National Association for the Advancement of Colored People
36. MRI - Magnetic resonance imaging

37. AFL-CIO - American Federation of Labor and Congress of Industrial Organization
38. NORAD - North American Aerospace Defense Command
39. UPC - Universal Product Code
40. ZIP (Code) - Zone Improvement Plan
41. M*A*S*H - Mobile Army Surgical Hospital
42. FEMA - Federal Emergency Management Agency
43. INTERPOL - International Criminal Police Organization
44. PM (Time) - Post Meridiem
45. AM (Time) - Ante Meridiem
46. SNAFU - Systems Normal, All Fouled Up
47. MO - Modus Operandi
48. NOAA - National Oceanic and Atmospheric Administration
49. ICBM (Military) - Intercontinental Ballistic Missile
50. HDMI - High-Definition Multimedia Interface

Alter Egos

1. Lady of the Lamp? Florence Nightingale
2. Baby Face Nelson? Lester Joseph Gillis
3. Angel of the Battlefield? Clara Barton
4. The Lizard King? Jim Morrison
5. Lady Rebecca? Pocahontas
6. Black Dahlia? Elizabeth Short
7. The Swamp Fox? Francis Marion
8. Papa Doc? President Duvalier of Haiti
9. The King of Swing? Benny Goodman
10. Black Swallow of Death? Eugene Bullard
11. Love Goddess? Rita Hayworth
12. The Red Baron? Manfred von Richthofen
13. The Nature Boy? Ric Flair
14. Scourge of God? Attila the Hun
15. The Flying Tomato? Shaun White
16. Godfather of Soul? James Brown
17. 50 Cent? Curtis Jackson III
18. The Admiral? David Robinson
19. Old Blood and Guts? General George Patton
20. Athens of the North? Edinburgh, Scotland
21. The Square Mile? London, England
22. The Golden Bear? Jack Nicklaus
23. Redd Foxx? John Elroy Sanford
24. Son of Sam? David Berkowitz

25. The Boss (Music)? Bruce Springsteen

26. The Say Hey Kid? Willie Mays

27. The Wizard of Menlo Park? Thomas Edison

28. Scarface? Al Capone

29. Black Swallow of Death? Eugene Bullard

30. The Man in Black? Johnny Cash

31. The First American? Benjamin Franklin

32. The Rock? Dwayne Johnson

33. Old Blue Eyes? Frank Sinatra

34. The Unabomber? Ted Kaczynski

35. The Duke? John Wayne

36. King of Cool? Steve McQueen

37. Austrian Oak? Arnold Schwarzenegger

38. The Blonde Bombshell? Marilyn Monroe

39. The British Bulldog? Winston Churchill

40. Little Bastard? James Dean

41. The Great Compromiser? Henry Clay

42. The Oracle of Omaha? Warren Buffett

43. First Lady of Song? Ella Fitzgerald

44. The Angel of Death? Josef Mengele

45. Dubya? President George W. Bush

46. The Good King? Henry IV of France

47. Big Al Jones? Albert Einstein

48. Daddy Long Legs? Fred Astaire

49. The Great One? Wayne Gretzky

50. The Iron Lady? Margaret Thatcher

Now that's Mythology

1. In Greek mythology, who was the personification of the rainbow? Iris

2. Who was the patron of Delphi? Apollo

3. In Norse mythology, what is the name of Thor's hammer? Mjolnir

4. In Egyptian mythology, who was god of the afterlife? Osiris

5. Who was the Greek god of dreams? Morpheus

6. Who are the first two humans in Norse mythology? Ask and Embla

7. Who was god of the sea in Roman mythology? Neptune

8. In Hindu mythology, who was the god of fire? Agni

9. Who was the goddess of love in Egyptian mythology? Hathor

10. In Greek mythology, who fired the arrow that hit Achilles in the heel? Paris

11. What Norse god had a spear named Gungnir? Odin

12. In Egyptian mythology, who had the head of an ibis and was the god of wisdom and magic? Thoth

13. Who was the Roman goddess of peace? Pax

14. In Greek mythology, who gave King Midas the power of turning everything he touched to gold? Dionysus

15. Asgard is one of how many worlds in Norse mythology? Nine

16. Who was leader of the Devas in Hindu mythology? Indra

17. In Norse mythology, who are the female helping spirits of Odin? Valkyrie

18. In Greek mythology, what was the Trojan Horse made of? Wood

19. In Norse mythology, who was the god of thunder? Thor

20. Who sired Pegasus in Greek mythology? Poseidon

21. In Roman mythology, who is the god of war? Mars

22. In Greek mythology, who was queen of the underworld? Persephone

23. In Egyptian mythology, who was the god of the Earth? Geb

24. Who did Heracles perform 12 impossible labors for? King Eurystheus

25. In Hindu mythology, who was the god of destruction? Shiva

26. Who was the mother of Thor in Norse mythology? Fjörgyn

27. In Roman mythology, who was the god of gates and beginnings? Janus

28. In Greek mythology, who was the King of Thebes? Oedipus

29. Who presides over the dead in Norse mythology? Hel

30. In Egyptian mythology, who was goddess of the sky and heavens? Nut

31. In Greek mythology, who was the goddess of beauty? Aphrodite

32. How many Titans were in Greek mythology? 12

33. What is the name of the weapon used by Poseidon? Trident

34. Who was known as a trickster and shape shifter in Norse mythology? Loki

35. What was the name of the prison for the Titans in Greek mythology? Tartarus

36. Who was called the "Dark One" in Hindu mythology? Matangi

37. Who was the goddess of love in Norse mythology? Freyja

38. In Greek mythology, who was the goddess of victory? Nike

39. In Norse mythology, what was the name of the female beings who ruled the destiny of gods and men? Norns

40. Who was the Hindu goddess of food and cooking? Annapurna

41. What goddess was represented with the head of a cat in Egyptian mythology? Bastet

42. In Norse mythology, who possessed the Gjallarhorn? Heimdallr

43. In Greek mythology, who opened a jar out of curiosity and let out all the evils of humanity? Pandora

44. In Egyptian mythology, who was the jackal-headed god associated with mummification? Anubis

45. In Roman mythology, who was the father of Jupiter? Saturn

46. In Greek mythology, how many daughters did Zeus have? 9

47. Who married her brother Osiris in Egyptian mythology? Isis

48. Who was known as "Mother of All" in Norse mythology? Frigg

49. In Hindu mythology, who was the god of death? Yama

50. In Egyptian mythology, who was known as the "Crocodile Goddess"? Ammit

Everything Under the Sun

1.   What is the name of the dog on the cover of Cracker Jacks? Bingo

2.   In what year was the video game *Pac-Man* released? 1980

3.   What is a Haboob? Dust storm

4.   What flower is also known as the Lent Lily? Wild Daffodil

5.   What is the sediment at the bottom of a wine barrel after fermentation called? Lees

6.   What does a Farrier do? Shoes horses

7.   What do the numbers on a standard dice add up to? 21

8.   What historical female was born Phoebe Moses? Anne Oakley

9.   What is the eighth sign of the Zodiac? Scorpio

10.   What clothing item did Louis Reard create in 1946? Bikini

11.   What does the P.T. stand for in P.T. Barnum? Phineas Taylor

12.   What was the first item sold on Ebay? Broken laser printer

13.   By what name is Lawrence Tureaud better known as? Mr. T

14.   How many rings are on the Audi car logo? Four

15.   Starbucks took its name from what novel? Moby Dick

16.   Martedi is Italian for which day of the week? Tuesday

17.   What company did Ingvar Kamprad start in 1943? IKEA

18.   What does the Q stand for in Q-tip? Quality

19. What is the name of the doctor who was convicted of involuntary manslaughter in the death of Michael Jackson? Conrad Murray

20. What super hero was modeled after Douglas Fairbanks Sr.? Superman

21. What is produced in a ginnery? Cotton

22. What was the only time Germans and Allies fought together in World War II? Battle for Castle Itter

23. In which country were LEGOS first produced? Denmark

24. What does a Cartomaniac collect? Maps

25. What was the first registered domain name? Symbolics.com

26. What are the dots on dice and dominos called? Pips

27. In chess, what piece always stays on the same color squares? Bishop

28. A Pontil is a metal rod used in what process? Glassblowing

29. What drink originates from the Arabic word Qahwa? Coffee

30. Which computer company was founded in 1983 as Control Video Corporation? AOL

31. What superhero owns Queen Industries? Green Arrow

32. Which day of the year is known as Star Wars Day? May 4

33. What vehicle model was nicknamed Tin Lizzie? Model T

34. What is someone who makes barrels or casks called? Cooper

35. Thomas the Tank Engine lives on which fictional island? Sodor

36. Pitman and Teeline are forms of what type of writing? Shorthand

37. Sevruga and Osetrove are varieties of what food? Caviar

38. Who was the first Eagle Scout to become U.S. President? John F. Kennedy

39. What is the world's number one traded commodity? Crude oil

40. How many squares are on an official Scrabble board? 225

41. Vichyssoise is a type of what food? Soup

42. How many days are in one fortnight? 14

43. How old was Marilyn Monroe when she died? 36

44. How many dominoes are in a standard domino set? 28

45. What is the smallest denomination of U.S. paper currency to not feature a U.S. President? $10 bill

46. What are the plastic things on the end of shoelaces called? Aglets

47. In what country was Pez Candy first introduced in 1927? Austria

48. How many squares are on a chess board? 64 (204 if you counted all possible combinations that form a square)

49. Someone born on December 18th has what zodiac symbol? Sagittarius

50. What color is the blood of insects? Yellow

51. What is the most expensive ever man-made object? International Space Station

52. What does the K stand for in Kmart? Kresge

53. How many rooms does the White House have? 132

54. How many dots are used in each letter in the Braille system? 6

55. What kind of nut is used to make pesto? Pine nut

56. How many ridges does a U.S. dime have? 118

57. In 1935, what was the first American beer to be sold in a can? Krueger's

58. What letter on a standard keyboard sits directly to the left of "C"? X

59. What creature appears on the flag of Wales? Red dragon

60. A woodpecker can peck up to how many times per second? 20

61. Which U.S. Constitutional Amendment guarantees a speedy public trial for criminal offenses? 6th Amendment

62. The perfume L'Interdit by Givenchy was created in 1957 for which actress? Audrey Hepburn

63. Who is the patron saint of music? Saint Cecilia

64. Who was Kim Kardashian's first husband? Damon Thomas

65. What is the most common insect on Earth? Beetle

66. What kind of bean is used to make hummus? Garbanzo

67. Arthur Curry is the real name of which super hero? Aquaman

68. How many Power Rangers made up the original team? 5

69. How many ridges does a U.S. quarter have? 119

70. Who was former U.S. Vice President Al Gore's freshman roommate at Harvard? Tommy Lee Jones

71. How many months of the year have only 30 days? 4

72. Elvis Presley collected statues of which famous female? Joan of Arc

73. What is the sum-total of all the numbers on a roulette wheel? 666

74. Who did Michael Jackson marry on May 26, 1994? Lisa Marie Presley

75. What company bought Bentley Motors in 1998? Volkswagen

76. What online company's original name was Cadabra.com? Amazon

77. What does the Latin phrase "Amor caecus est" translate to in English? Love is blind

78. What type of food is Booyah? Stew

79. What is the name of Superman's birth mom? Lara

80. What day of the year signifies the start of Lent? Ash Wednesday

81. What was the first cartoon character to have been made into a balloon for a parade? Felix the Cat

82. What is the least used letter in the English alphabet? Q

83. What is the first name of astronaut Buzz Aldrin? Edwin

84. In what country did the kilt originate? Scotland

85. What country is the world's largest producer of rubies? Myanmar

86. Who was Miss Hungary in 1936? Zsa Zsa Gabor

87. What object is also known as Tavernier Blue? Hope Diamond

88. Which Mexican drink is made from the Agave plant? Tequila

89. In which U.S. state was Microsoft founded? New Mexico

90. Alcea is the genus name for which flowering plant? Hollyhock

91. Lechon is a dish made with what kind of meat? Pork

92. What country's legislative body is called the Diet? Japan

93. What was the first name of Kentucky Fried Chicken founder, Colonel Sanders? Harland

94. What was Elvis Presley's only commercial endorsement? Southern Maid Doughnuts

95. What type of gem is the Star of India? Sapphire

96. How many gallons of beer are in a furkin? 9

97. What is the largest Native American tribe in the United States? Cherokee

98. Who sculpted *The Thinker*? Auguste Rodin

99. In what year was the first edition of the video game *Doom* released? 1993

100. In which year was the New York City ballet founded? 1948

101. What is the world's tallest type of grass? Giant bamboo

102. What fruit has the most protein? Avocado

103. How many cards is each player initially dealt in a game of Texas Hold'em? 2

104. Who was the first female country singer to win a Grammy Award? Dottie West

105. What is the last word in the *Bible's* "New Testament"? Amen

106. How many stars are on the car logo for Subaru? 6

107. What is another name for a Lexicon? Dictionary

108. Who is the only 20th century U.S. President on Mt. Rushmore? Teddy Roosevelt

109. What is the eleventh letter of the Greek alphabet? Lambda

110. The mythical creature Niseag is better known by what name? Loch Ness Monster

111. How many colored squares are on a Rubik's Cube? 54

112. What has been the most common first name of U.S. First Lady's? Elizabeth

113. What does the U.S. Marine Corps motto, "Semper Fidelis" mean? Always Faithful

114. Who is actress Mariska Hargitay's mother? Jayne Mansfield

115. What fruit is the main ingredient in the liquor Quetsch? Plum

116. What is the name of the Israeli Secret Service? Mossad

117. What is the tip of an umbrella called? A Ferrule

118. What is a chef's hat called? Toque or Dodin Bouffant

119. In what year, did Twitter debut? 2006

120. What was the original price of *Action Comics* #1 which featured Superman for the first time? 10 cents

121. What is the rarest color for a diamond? Green

122. What is the longest English word without a vowel? Rhythm

123. What breed of dog is cartoon character Snoopy? Beagle

124. Ojani Noa was the first husband of which entertainer? Jennifer Lopez

125. What does the L.L. stand for in L.L. Bean? Leon Leonwood

126. In what country was Alexander Graham Bell born? Scotland

127. What is Gynophobia the fear of? Women

128. How many dice are used to play Yahtzee? 5

129. What is the only fruit which has its seeds on the outside? Strawberry

130. From what mineral is pencil lead made of? Graphite

131. What material traditionally represents a third wedding anniversary? Leather

132. What is the official name for the Beefeaters at the Tower of London? Yeoman of the Guard

133. What type of food are Roquefort and Emmentaler? Cheese

134. How many letters are in "Supercalifragilisticexpialidocious"? 34

135. What is the shortest word in the English language with three Y's? Syzygy

136. How many playing spaces does a standard Connect Four game have? 42

137. How many possible landing spaces are there on a roulette wheel? 38

138. What company produced the first handheld calculator? Texas Instruments

139. Which month was named after the Roman god of war? March

140. What is the most widely spoken language in the world? Chinese Mandarin

141. What is the only female name used in the NATO Phonetic Alphabet? Juliette

142. What is the only vowel not on the top line of a standard keyboard? A

143. Barbara Gordon is the real name of which super hero? Batgirl

144. Which wedding anniversary is traditionally referred to as the Coral wedding anniversary? 35th

145. What does a Phillumenist collect? Matchboxes

146. What is the national flower of France? Iris

147. How long is each term for the Secretary-General of the United Nations? 5 years

148. What is the name of Dennis the Menace's dog? Gnasher

149. How many white stripes are on the U.S. Flag? 6

150. Which Academy Award winning actress was once actress Carrie Fisher's step-mom? Elizabeth Taylor

151. What root is used to flavor root beer? Sarsaparilla

152. How many stocks comprise the Dow Jones Industrial Average? 30

153. What color is a Peridot stone? Green

154. What was the world's first hotel chain? Hilton

155. In what year was Coca-Cola first introduced? 1886

156. How many letters are in the Hawaiian alphabet? 13

157. What plant's byproducts are used to make rum? Sugarcane

158. What does a Funambulist do? Tightrope Walker

159. What color light is displayed from the port side of a ship? Red

160. What is the study of tissue cells? Histology

161. What is the indentation at the bottom of a wine bottle called? Punt

162. What fruit is also called a Chinese gooseberry? Kiwi

163. How many sheets are in a ream of paper? 500

164. Lycanthropy is the ability to turn into what creature? Werewolf

165. In which country was Arnold Schwarzenegger born? Austria

166. The first toilet paper had what added to it to act as a lubricant? Aloe

167. What car company released the Dictator in 1927? Studebaker

168. Who was on the June 27, 1994 cover of *Time*? O.J. Simpson

169. How many holes are on a classic cribbage board? 121

170. What company made the Amiga 4000 computer? Commodore

171. Who did actress Vivien Leigh marry on August 31, 1940? Laurence Olivier

172. What animal is the symbol for the Capricorn zodiac sign? Goat

173. What day of the year is Sadie Hawkins Day? February 29th

174. What does M&M stand for on its candy wrappers? Mars & Murrie

175. In what year was the first Rotary Club founded? 1905

176. What is the world's smallest tree? Greenland Dwarf Willow

177. In what year was the first email sent? 1971

178. What word has the most definitions in the English language? Set

179. What is the Italian word for bartender? Barista

180. Granny Smith, Golden Delicious and Gala are all examples of which fruit? Apple

181. Which tree produces acorns? Oak

182. What did Harrison Ford do for a living before becoming an actor? Carpenter

183. What percentage of a cucumber is water? 96%

184. Who did Bobby Fischer defeat in 1972 to become the first American World Chess Champion? Boris Spassky

185. What is added to white sugar to make brown sugar? Molasses

186. At what age's birthday party was President John F. Kennedy when Marilyn Monroe sang him *Happy Birthday*? 46

187. In what year was the first iPhone released? 2007

188. What vehicle brand was the first to install brakes in 1849? Volvo

189. In what year, did Walt Disney World open? 1971

190. What entertainer's real name is Ehrich Weiss? Houdini

191. Who did actress Julia Roberts marry in 1993? Lyle Lovett

192. What type of milk is traditional feta cheese made from? Sheep's milk

193. What was the first country to use police dogs? Scotland

194. In what year did the first Wal-Mart open? 1962

195. The cashew is native to which country? Brazil

196. Based on total volume, what is the world's largest pyramid? Cholula

197. In which U.S. state is Brown University located? Rhode Island

198. In what year did the New York City subway open? 1904

199. How many pawns does each player have at the start of a chess game? 8

200. What is the largest gland in the human body? Liver

Thank you all very much.

Thank you to my son Dylan for being an awesome kid.

Thank you to my parents for teaching me what hard work means.

Thank you to the brave men and women who serve and protect my freedom.

Thank you to Gary Vaynerchuk for showing me how to do what I love.

Thank you to James Altucher for teaching me how to choose myself.

And thank you to everyone who read this book.

Made in the USA
San Bernardino, CA
26 January 2018